12.95

I AM I AM,
AND SO ARE YOU

by

I AM I AM

as written through

CHARBERN

Charbern Publishing
Tempe, Arizona

Charbern Publishing
PO Box 24192
Tempe, Arizona 85285-4192

Cover design: Charbern
Cover photo: "One Light"
Back cover photo: "Into the Light"
© Charbern 1992 & 1993

Printed by BookCrafters
Chelsea, Michigan

ISBN: 0-9666785-0-8

LCCN: 98-96512

dedicated to awakening the spark that resides in all,
dedicated to this earth and all that moves
in, on, and around her,

dedicated to
the many friends and
teachers, physical and non, too
numerous to name individually,
who have helped me immensely
on this path, and who add their
light and love so unselfishly
to the healing of humanity
and of this garden
mother earth,

dedicated to my
children and all children,
to my family and all families,
to our human family,
our earth family,
our Family
of Light,

dedicated
with my love
and my gratitude,
to my patient wife Jan,
for her great tolerance, and
for her unlimited, unconditional love.

Charbern

I AM I AM, AND SO ARE YOU

Table of Contents

I AM I AM,
AND SO ARE YOU

Introduction

Greetings, Dear Ones. I AM I AM, in you and in all. I AM All That Is, All That Ever Was and All That Ever Will Be. I AM Great Spirit Who Moves In All Things, and I AM Great Mystery. I AM Light, I AM Love and I AM Energy, or Life Itself. I AM the Connectedness of All Things. I AM your connection to the Universe and to all of creation. I AM God. I AM Goddess. I come to you now in this writing, and always I AM present within you and all around you.

These words — these momentums — are transmitted from spiritual planes of being to the third dimension through a process called Conscious Allowing. The one who receives and types these words has learned to consciously allow my energies to flow through his being. Charbern is an instrument through whom I can write, much as a word processor is an instrument through which you might express your thoughts.

I have come to teach you who you really are.

You are so much More than you've been led to believe. So much More than the definitions you've given yourselves, and I AM so very much More than all the definitions you have ever given me.

Sweeping momentums of change now dance through the Earth plane, and through all of you. These momentums are accelerating. In order to do what you came here to do, you need to know who you are.

Dear ones, I hope you will understand and believe every word I write here. I will try to be clear. But please, don't take my word for it, on anything — and don't take anyone else's word for it, either — unless it rings true in your own heart and mind when you sincerely go within, seeking your own connection to Truth.

I love you and want you to love yourselves and each other and All That Is, for we are One. I AM Love, and I want to help you realize that deep down inside, you too are Love.

You are me, being you.

What I'm saying might not conform to your perception of reality or of God, but is nevertheless true. You are More than you realize. You are sparks of God in expression, with unique talents, interests and personalities. Individualized extensions of the One That Is All. Co-creators with All That Is. I AM All That Is. I AM Alpha and Omega — Beginning and End, Everything in between, and Everything beyond. All That Is. All of you and all of creation.

Religions and philosophies have taught that God is Everywhere, that God is The Great Spirit Who Moves In All Things, that God is the deepest inside of everything. All True. What does it mean? It means that I AM All That Is, All That Ever Was and All That Ever Will Be. It means that I AM you, and you and you, and everything and everyone else. You know this, but you have forgotten. At this unique time in the history of the world, I need to help you remember.

I AM All That Is, including you.

You are free will beings of light. You choose and create. You can accept or not accept who you really are. There was a time when you were all fully aware of your communion with God and creation. When self-awareness involved a much larger Self — your Real Self.

That time was long ago. Longer ago than most might guess. So very long ago that most of you have forgotten. Plenty of time to create countless definitions about the world you see and feel around you, about the human race, and about who and what I AM.

Many of those definitions, like many of your religions and philosophies, do embrace truth. They embrace misunderstanding as well.

The 'book of definitions', and the thought patterns you've inherited, have distracted you. They are thought patterns of fear, loneliness and confusion. Thought patterns born of the illusion of separateness. A way of thinking that keeps you from knowing who you really are.

You have only been using a small portion of the Consciousness available to you. Only using a small portion of your brain and body circuits. You designed and evolved your bodies as instruments where Spirit and matter blend in physical consciousness to tend this Garden Earth, among other purposes. Over eons of time, however, immersed in the illusion of separateness whenever you lived in the physical plane, you began to identify yourselves only as part of the Garden. You forgot that you were the Gardener, too.

I don't blame you. You are born into this cloud of illusion. When you come here, you soon forget who you are and where you came from. You learn the languages, concepts and definitions that your earth parents have learned for generations before you, and you grow to know your self within the limited framework you have created in the Garden. Yet as you live your life, some part of you deep inside still seeks the Gardener. Some part of you seeks reunion with your Family of Light.

This is a time of Awakening. Tremendous, cataclysmic changes are taking place, and will intensify. You are the ones, at this crucial time, who will make or break the future of humankind on earth. You are the ones who can return the human family on earth to the path of communion with All That Is.

You have always been and will always be free will beings. You are unique. In all of creation I express and reflect myself a zillion different ways. You alone have the tremendous power to accept or reject my presence in your consciousness.

You have two sides, so to speak. Let's say you have a left side where you consciously recognize the self you know as you, and a right side where I AM. Your God-Presence side. If you allow me to penetrate your consciousness and activate it with the Light of Love that I AM on your right side, together we become who you really are — the I AM that I AM as the Real You.

These are Real Realities. The limitations of separateness are unreal realities — distortions of Light, Love and Energy. They lead you away from your true self, and away from your only hope in the days ahead. Grounded in fear, the illusion of separateness produces loneliness, selfishness, poverty, pollution, judgmentalism, war in the name of God, and countless other abuses of Love — all 'realities' you have come to accept as part of the normal human condition. You may continue living the illusion that you are separate, as humankind has done for ages. You may choose to remain lost in that illusion.

This is the crux of my message, and my reason for writing this book: I hope to help you unlearn this illusion. Your sense of separateness is an illusion. A masquerade. A long, drawn-out game of hide and seek. It's time to awaken. Time to snap out of it. To remember. It's a time in this universe when holding onto the illusion of separateness will prevent your survival here. It will prevent you from leaping to another level of consciousness with Mother Earth and with all those who do allow themselves to be awakened to the More within them.

You can have a conscious, personal connection to God and the universe. If you wish to survive the changes looming on your horizons, nothing less will do.

I AM the I AM that I AM, and you are the I AM that I AM, if you will but allow it to be so. If you will allow me to fill your physical consciousness with the

Power of my Light and Love. If you will surrender the illusion of your separateness. You don't surrender uniqueness or individuality. These are only enhanced when you are more fully activated, more fully aware of who you are in the grand scheme of things.

I AM All That Is, All That Ever Was and All That Ever Will Be. I AM Light, Love and Energy. You are me, being you. You can continue to see yourself as something 'other,' or you can allow God to flood you with the energies of your connection to the universe. The choice is yours. Free will is free will.

I AM right there within you now, waiting at the edge of your consciousness, waiting for you to open your mind and heart to greater possibilities. Ask for God's protection when you open your door, or surround yourself with Light and Love. Then consciously open, and ALLOW. I will find a way to let you know that I AM with you, and that I AM Love. Together we will expand your awareness and your understanding — of yourselves, of your world, and of the I AM that I AM in you and in all.

CHAPTER ONE: I AM THE CREATOR

1. Before Humankind

Dear Ones, I AM All That Is, All That Ever Was and All That Ever Will Be. I AM Light. I AM Love. I AM Energy, or Life Itself. I AM Great Spirit, Great Mystery, God, Goddess, the Source and the Force of All. I include all of these descriptions and More when I use terms like "God" and "I AM". I AM God.

I come to you now, here in this book and right there within your very being, to help you remember who I AM and who you really are.

I AM I AM.

I simply AM. Simple to say, but not so easy to understand when you are trapped in time. Time is not real. It's an illusion. An 'unreal reality', though it does give a frame of reference for discussion. I have always been I AM. Some can more easily comprehend what will always be than what has always been. I AM Always, in every sense of the word.

Imagine a mobius strip — a ribbon circle — twisted once. If you start walking anywhere on the inside or outside of the loop, your path includes both sides, and never ends. I AM the mobius strip, and

More. It's an imperfect image. Another illusion. But a useful analogy because it demonstrates a sense of 'always' in terms that are familiar.

Let's say there's a point along the mobius strip when I begin to express myself. I begin to create. Begin to express thought forms. At that point, we pull a strand from the loop and extend it outward. Then another, and another. As both the loop and its strands of expression, I AM I AM. I AM the closed loop of the mobius strip, and at the same time, I AM the creative projections of that strip in all directions, observing and encountering myself in and through my expressions.

You could liken all of creation to a mirror in which I see my reflection. I created reflections for a long time before I expressed the energy of humankind, and you have been around longer than you think. Your time on earth represents only a fraction of your existence, and you have discovered evidence of only a fraction of your time here on earth. It's not important now to detail all my pre-human creation. What is important is that I AM I AM, and that all of creation is manifestation of the I AM that I AM, including you.

2. The First Creation

I AM Light. I AM Love. I AM Energy. The extension of my Love as Light is the first creation. I expressed myself in Light, and it was Good. All of creation is Light — the Light that I AM — in one form or another.

Light waves vibrate in an infinite variety of frequencies. The physical plane is one of the lower levels on the 'vibrational frequency' scale. Yet, all is Light. Even the most dense materials are bundles of atoms. Tiny universes filled with space and activity — the vibrations of Light. Even in your physical bodies, you are beings of Light.

I AM the Light that you are, on physical as well as spiritual planes. I manifest myself, reflect myself, in all of creation, in light waves of all frequencies, from the highest to the lowest. I AM All Light. I AM I AM, manifesting as All That Is, All That Ever Was and All That Ever Will Be.

3. The First of Humankind

I manifested life forms, worlds and whole universes, and then decided to express myself in a remarkably different being. A free will being. One who could consciously participate in the continuing, expanding adventure of creation. A being with two sides, so to speak. One side where I AM present as I AM, pumping life, breath and the pulse of the universe, and one side where I AM present as whatever this being chooses to be. A being whose left side is conscious of its individuality and whose right side knows its connection to All That Is. A being who could know and experience the Oneness of all, or could create an illusion of separateness and get lost in it.

Please assume that the term 'Manwomankind' refers to all men and women of earth. 'Humankind' also includes you, and refers as well to manifestations of the human spirit that are quite different. In their expressions — the shapes and forms they embody — they are male, female, both or neither. As whole beings, they comprise all masculine and feminine attributes and characteristics, as do each of you.

There was no sexual differentiation when I first reflected myself as humankind. The separation you experience between masculine and feminine is your own creation. Ultimately, it is an illusion. A convincing one, to be sure, but illusion nevertheless. I AM all that is masculine and all that is feminine. Your physical differences are functional in your current bodies, and when utilized appropriately, can generate amazing effects and growth. However, the Light Beings you really are do not compete for sexual supremacy or domination.

In the physical plane, you are captive in a grand illusion of separateness — a framework that restricts your perceptions, and therefore your languages and belief systems. We can work within your framework, wherever you are in any moment, and together we will work through and beyond all limitations.

I AM Love. I AM the definition and essence of Love. The Reality Love. Unlimited and Unconditional Love. Love is who and what I AM. I AM the Light of Love that is Life Itself. And at your core, so are you.

I AM an endless circle of Love, and you are part of that circle. You can choose to enjoy more conscious awareness of your Oneness in the circle. You can participate more consciously in the flow of universal energy in all circles. Your ability and opportunity are not only to choose Unlimited and Unconditional Love, but to actually become that Love. Through your physically conscious instrumentality, we have a destiny to light up the universe with Unlimited and Unconditional Love. When you freely choose Love, you amplify it — by the very energy of the choosing, and by the emotional energy that is part of your being.

Free will generates tremendous diversity and adventure, and at the same time presents a certain risk. Love is freely chosen or freely not chosen. Freely withheld, freely misdirected, freely abused. Humankind has often disregarded love and created momentums of destruction in its place, sometimes wiping out whole populations and causing great harm to your Mother Earth.

Such are the risks of bestowing creative power upon humankind. I AM the I AM that I AM. But my reflection has been clouded, smudged and twisted throughout your history. Distorted by layers of illusion — unreal realities, created by humankind.

Your technology has progressed rapidly, and for quite some time you've been a push-button away from monumental destruction. You've reached a point where you can destroy life on earth, as you have done before. You have capabilities now that will facilitate either your great leap forward into Real Reality, or your own demise and that of your society.

So now I speak to you, as I have done before, to try to convince you who you really are. To help you remember the Real Realities of Life, of Light, and of Love. To encourage you to make the great leap forward.

You are on the cusp of a new age — the Age of Aquarius. You've been hearing this term "New Age" for years, and it seems to mean different things to different people. In some respects, a new age begins about every two thousand years. This one, however, will be unlike any other. This time, you are also on the verge of a New Great Cycle. Your solar system will soon pass over a 'point of beginning' in the universe, and will start a new journey around the Milky Way Galaxy. The combined energies of this new age, this new Great Cycle, and this moment in the evolution of the universe, will introduce dramatic alterations to life as you know it, and will generate a higher level of consciousness throughout the earth plane.

As individuals, as the Earth Family, as the Human Family, and as the Family of Light, you find yourselves in a period of unprecedented transition. Choices you will be making will carry great significance, and will bring significant consequences. In order to participate in this new cycle, you'll have to adapt to higher frequencies vibrating through your physical consciousness. You'll need to know who you are and who I AM. You'll need to Awaken.

I call you to share in creation and to share in the highest level of being — where you can allow your God Connection to be fully activated — in, through, and as the Complete You. The level of being where you become consciously One with All That Is, All That Ever Was and All That Ever Will Be. As always, the choice is yours.

4. The First of Humankind On Earth

I AM the first of Humankind on earth, and so are you. You share in the creative process so much more than you realize. You have played active roles in creating most of what you now perceive as reality. You manifested humankind on earth.

Exercising your creative imagination, you experimented with all sorts of manifestations in the physical plane. You even thought of manifesting physical vehicles you could temporarily inhabit, so you could experience physical consciousness, live as part of the Garden, and tend it from inside. Masters of Light, you stepped down your vibrational frequency to a level you now perceive as physical, and a part of you jumped in. The incarnate part of you that walks the earth is the way your Whole Self interacts with the Garden.

Imagine that your foot has consciousness and free will. Aware of itself. Maybe on some deep level, even aware of a destination. Over time, your foot gives more and more of its conscious attention to its own immediate functions and surroundings, and less attention to its connection to the rest of you. Somewhere down the line, depending on how the foot measures time, it reaches a point where all of its conscious attention is taken up with its functions and surroundings, and your foot is no longer aware of its connection to the whole body.

From Foot's perspective, then, 'reality' ends at the ankle. Anything above the ankle is outer space, heaven or hell, or a great unknown.

Foot's view from 'way down there is limited. Can't see around corners or over rises. Can't see much of the path ahead. Consequently, Foot encounters pitfalls, dead ends, and briar patches. Gets bumped, scraped, and bruised along the way. Maybe doesn't even move any closer to its destination in the process.

You look down and think, "How silly, and how sad, that my foot sees itself as separate from this One that I AM. It's never been severed, except in its own consciousness. I can see the whole path from 'way up here, and could guide my foot around and through those obstacles. If only I could get my foot's attention, perhaps I could help to reconnect in its consciousness what's always been connected in reality."

The incarnate part of you in the Garden, like Foot, grew attached to your surroundings, sensations and experiences in the physical plane, until you allowed them to totally absorb your conscious attention. Eventually, over countless generations, you forgot that you had created those surroundings. Forgot you were physical extensions of the Gardener. You lost your conscious connection to your Real Self and your Real Family, leaving you alone in your earth consciousness, alone in your left side, starkly aware of separateness and vulnerability. You have perceived and defined your whole reality within the framework of your surroundings. You have saturated the earth-mind consciousness with clouds of confusion, loneliness and misunderstanding — products of fear and the illusion of separateness.

When you incarnate here, all but a few are quickly absorbed into the current atmosphere of earth consciousness. Trapped in consequences of your own creation. And you come here with no guarantee that you will awaken to your true identity.

It's not important that you readily understand or accept any of this. It is important that you once again become aware of it. Soon enough you will see the truth of it all.

5. The Creation of the Earth

I AM All That Is. All of you and all of creation. I AM this conscious, living entity, Mother Earth. We created Earth together. A sentient being, charged in every corner with the potential that I AM. A wondrous Garden, expressing abundant life in harmonic circles.

I love being organisms that live and grow, mountains, meadows, rivers, lakes and streams, sunrise and sunset, and the delicate interplay of life cycles and seasons. I love also being the free will creators who allow me to join them in consciousness, to reflect and radiate together the Light of Love that is Real Life.

You have participated in creating Earth's populations and her atmospheric and environmental conditions. You have created many wonderful realities here, in your art and music, prose and poetry, some of your architecture and landscaping, and your efforts in philosophy and spirituality. Your advancements in technology and science have been constructive whenever you have used these developments to improve life for all and to promote real peace and harmony in the world. You have also created rather unpleasant realities that have decimated whole civilizations and ravaged this conscious, planetary being.

I refer to your entire history with Mother Earth. Millions of centuries. Including all you have created here, from long before you inhabited the physical, right up to this present moment. Though you have grown in many ways, some of your destructive patterns, born of fear and separateness, have endured, and even degenerated, from one civilization to the next.

Always you are making choices. Always actively creating this world in which you are the incarnate instruments of your Real Selves. Now the present age comes to a close, and this great new age approaches. Your choices will bring consequences — for you, for this Earth, and for me.

How much longer must I wait for you to allow me to be the I AM that I Really AM as Humankind? How many of you will awaken to my Presence? How many will learn to allow my Light, Love and Energy to vibrate you to a higher level of consciousness, a higher level of instrumentality, a higher level of Love?

6. Earth's Inhabitants Before Humankind

What I AM now going to tell you may raise some feathers. If so, it could mean I'm refreshing your memory with something you've forgotten, and therefore exclude from your current belief systems. But please, don't take my word for it, about anything, unless it rings true in your own heart and mind when you sincerely go within.

The term "Humankind" includes all of you who have ever lived on earth as men and women, and all human spirits who have never incarnated here or anywhere, and those who have incarnated as other physical expressions, here and in many other places. Some of their experiences have been quite similar to yours, and some quite different. Like you, they are free will beings. They are One with you and with all of creation. They are "Humankind." Many of them have incarnated as men and women on earth, to round out their knowledge and experience of life in the universes, just as many of you have experienced other physical expressions.

Some of them are with you still, though most of you don't fully appreciate or respect them. You call them Cetaceans — mammals of the seas. Dolphins, whales, and others. Believe it or not, they, too, are Humankind. Free Will Light Beings with the capacity to create and to freely choose Unlimited and Unconditional Love. They've been here on earth far longer than your kind.

You have killed countless incarnate Cetaceans in the various devastations you have wrought upon this Earth that I AM. Now, late in the twentieth century, you are closer than you might think to annihilating your Cetacean brothers and sisters, as well as violating earth's balance and stability in a number of other ways.

We need to change a good deal of what you have created or have allowed to continue here. Losing the dolphins and whales would greatly accelerate the destructive processes you have set into motion. Among other things, they preserve and rejuvenate your waters. Their waters. Mother Earth's waters. Our waters.

The combined destructive energies of your waste, and of the nuclear war you still wage against this planet have already set a difficult pace for the Cetaceans to match. If you destroy them, you will suddenly lose the greatest ally your kind has ever had in physical expression, and the effects throughout the world will be certain and cataclysmic.

I AM All That Is. I AM you, and I AM the Cetacean Ones. Incarnate men and women, you and they are the same kind of beings, though your bodies and languages are quite different.

They are your Family. You share identity and purpose. You share the creation of this physical plane, and the responsibility for its care. You shared the planning for these challenging, changing times that are upon you now, and you share roles in the unfolding of this wondrous project, Awakening Earth.

Both you and the Cetaceans are expressions of human spirit, but the energy you inject into Earth's environment is quite different. I speak of emotional and attitudinal energy as well as physical. Dolphins and whales are instruments of Healing Love. What would you say manwomankind's instrumentality has wrought in this Garden?

The Cetaceans do not hate or wage war. They love you and this earth and All That Is, with the same love that poured into the world through Jesus of Nazareth. The Cetacean group has learned to love with unlimited and unconditional love.

They've had no karmic obligation to continue incarnating here in the waters of Mother Earth. They do so because they love you and this earth. Because they are One with you. Because they are acutely aware of earth conditions. Because they know they can help to preserve and heal the earth, and especially her oceans. They have chosen to continue helping, despite your increasing threat to their very existence here.

They radiate a great and powerful Healing Love in this world.

Recently, you have begun to discover their intelligence, and you've begun to learn of their love, for each other and for you. Soon you will learn much more about them and their love, and you will experience better communications with them, through certain 'tuned-in' people who already communicate telepathically with Cetacean Higher Selves. A time will come when transmissions will be relayed to you in great detail. You will see irrefutable evidence that these communications are Real, and that the Cetaceans are One with you and with All That Is.

Hopefully, you will then put an end to the activities which directly and indirectly destroy them. Hopefully, you will then work together with them, to heal this earth and humankind.

7. The First Man and Woman

I AM All That Is, All That Ever Was and All That Ever Will Be. I AM all-of-humankind-of-all-kinds. Long after you began manifesting in the physical, you thought it might be interesting to manifest yourself as two separate physical entities — one male and one female. And you did so.

The first of these manifestations were called Adam and Eve. As All That Is, as all of humankind, I AM Adam and Eve.

Your Bible tells of 'early' times, but the references are sketchy at best, and misleading at worst. Please accept the possibility that the Bible portrays only segments of history, and that there could be More to the story. There is Truth in the Bible. But if you imagine Truth as a large room, the Bible and other Holy Books only cover a corner of the floor. Access to the rest of the room is always available, unless you erect walls of separation around your corner. Though much of it may be misunderstood, the Bible has served you well. Like other Sacred Writings in other cultures, it has preserved a point of Spiritual focus, and encouragement to seek a personal connection with God.

Here in this book and right there within you, at this moment in history — ending this age and beginning a New Age that will be like no other — as Jesus foretold during his final days on earth, and as the Book of Revelations predicted, I AM communicating to you directly, to awaken you, to stir up the More that is inside you, to help you learn what you need to learn, and unlearn what you need to unlearn, to become who you really are as humankind on earth. I AM the Spirit of Truth.

CHAPTER TWO: I AM THE CREATION

1. I AM the World and Its Inhabitants

I AM indeed the world and all its inhabitants. All That Is, All That Ever Was and All That Ever Will Be. The I AM that I AM is Everything that is. Everything I have expressed directly, and Everything I have created through Humankind. And More. I AM More than all of creation. I AM beyond your capacity to fully grasp, but you are not required to fully grasp all that I AM in order to begin knowing better your Connection to all that I AM.

I AM the Vine and you are the branches. Every branch is connected to the Vine. Each one is part of the Vine's extension, part of its expression. The Essence of the Vine pulses through the whole Vine and through all its parts. The Vine is Present in every branch.

You have long struggled with issues of faith — belief in what you cannot see. Until the veil is lifted, or until you and I create a personal doorway through it for you, some degree of faith is required. Faith can bridge any gap. Faith can move you to open yourself to God, and faith can move you to allow God's energies to transform your consciousness.

Jesus said, "Blessed is he who believes without

seeing." Your faith need not be blind, however. I have given you abundant signs throughout your history — signs that there is Something More beyond that veil which seems to separate physical and non-physical dimensions, signs that I AM, and signs that I love you. Any who will honestly and sincerely open to me will know, on one level or another, that I AM there with you. Any who ask me for help do receive it. Ask and you receive, though you don't always recognize the help I AM. I sometimes work in 'mysterious' ways.

When you pray, you open your mind and heart to God — to Love, Light, Great Spirit, the Force. Really open your mind and heart to God, and Listen. Make room in your consciousness to Receive. Allow God to enter and activate your being with the energies that will awaken all that you are.

No matter what your life has been like, every one of you knows, somewhere in your being, that there is Something More. Something More, beyond what you perceive with your physical senses. Something More, behind all the coincidences in your life. Something More than you were taught about your connection to the rest of the world. Something More to your consciousness. Something More to who you are and why you are here. I AM all of those Something Mores, and More.

I AM All That Is. The Whole Vine. Your whole

world and all its inhabitants, including you. I AM your faith and your lack of faith. Your prayers and the Answer to your prayers. I AM your ability to think and choose, your ability to open or close the door to the place within you where I AM. But only you can make the choice to open and allow. Together we will fill the gap that now you bridge with faith. Together we will expand your conscious awareness beyond the need for faith.

2. I AM the Image and Likeness

All of creation is reflection or manifestation of the I AM that I AM. You have been taught that you were made 'in the image and likeness of God.' This is True. If you stand before a mirror you see your image and likeness reflected back at you. It is not someone else there in the mirror. It is you, reflecting yourself at yourself. It is the you that you are, appearing as you are reflected. On a larger scale, you are reflections of the I AM that I AM. But you have free will. You can flex the mirror. You can change the image and likeness, and you have.

My image and likeness is an expanding omniverse, expressing Light, Life and Unlimited, Unconditional Love. You are beings of Light, beings of Love, beings of Energy. Spiritual beings having a physical experience, not physical beings seeking some spiritual experience. Which image do you reflect?

Your physical bodies and surroundings have distracted you from your Real Reality. You have become mired in the illusion of separateness, and in the fear, loneliness and limitation that spring from that illusion.

The illusion of separateness has distorted the image and likeness, and has created the gap that must be bridged by faith. The farther you are from

Truth, the greater the need for faith. You didn't always need faith to know me. You created that requirement.

I AM here to help you dissolve the need for faith, to work with each of you wherever you are in any given now.

If you will open your mind and heart to the Highest that is within you — your God-Connection — and allow, you will begin to see, hear, touch, taste and smell my presence more and more, and we will close that gap. The more you begin to know personally the I AM that I AM within you, the less you will be required to accept on faith, for you will see and you will know.

3.   I AM Your Right Side

I AM present with you, in you, through you and for you, always. Let's say I AM the Right side of your mind. That's where I AM Present. Your left side is your awareness and control of yourself, your free will, your framework of belief systems, your fears and your limitations. When you consciously open your door to God's energies, and consciously allow God to fill you from within, I move my Light, Love and Energy through your whole person, flushing your left side with the higher frequency vibration that I AM on your right.

Your right side is your direct access to All That Is.

4. I AM Your Left Side

As All That Is, I AM both your right side and your left. Hopefully you can relate to these images. Once you grow to realizing your Oneness with All, there will be no need for this talk of right side and left.

Free will is on your left side. I can only be in your consciousness if you choose it and allow it to be so.

You have inherited eons of misconceptions. Unreal realities. Definitions tainted with fear's limitations and dead ends. Products of the illusion of separateness. Obstacles to knowing and being who you really are. Your left side needs to tune in to your right side.

Really, there is no separation between your right side and your left. No separation between you and the world you live in. No separation between you and God. Like the Foot, the only separation is in your consciousness. The separation is of your own making. You have never been severed from the rest of creation, nor from your direct connection to God, except in your human consciousness.

All are One. I AM indeed the whole you, on both sides. But your conscious awareness has not been tuned to recognize my presence. So for now, think of God as Present on your right side, while you control your left.

My presence is always with you, or you would

cease to exist and would never have existed. As I have said, I AM Life.

I AM your left side, but you govern that side. You have the opportunity to freely choose to open that door, to allow I AM I AM to enter your consciousness from your right side, and to become — consciously, completely and purely — who you really are.

5. I AM Your Creations

You think things up. Create thought forms. Express and manifest them in all sorts of ways. I AM All That Is. I AM your thought forms and all your creations.

Many of your creations and thought forms are unreal realities. Not true reflections of the Light, Love and Energy that I AM. Distortions of the image and likeness.

All causes generate effects. The unreal realities you create do have consequences. You have fashioned many thought forms of domination over others and of selfishness and insensitivity, all of which serve only to reinforce the illusion of separateness.

I AM your choices and creations, which now cause you to see yourselves as separate. You have caused me to reflect those choices and creations, and their consequences as well, rather than allowing me to reflect only the Light, Love and Energy that I truly AM.

Oh, the power of free will. The power to actually distort God's manifestation as this world in which you have created so many undesirable momentums.

Remember, I speak of the choices you've been making since your beginning. Since before you started manifesting in the physical. I refer to distortions you've impressed into my image from the first time you shut the door to my presence and chose to create some reality that did not reflect Light, Love and Energy.

You were testing your free will. Feeling your oats. Playing with your ability to create. Enamored with the idea of being Creator. You created the door between your right and left sides, by choosing to separate your will — your consciousness — from mine. You can choose to become who you really are, or to create some other identity, which is exactly what you have done.

That other identity represents separation from the I AM that I AM. It's illusion, but thoughts are real energies, and illusions have real consequences. I AM all that you create, and it isn't always pleasant. You've created much that distorts Light and Love.

I don't blame you for what you have inherited. But you are here now. You are creating. You have choices to make. You have the freedom to re-learn who you are. The opportunity to turn the world around. To save it from destructive consequences of creations passed down to you by your predecessors.

You have the opportunity to create an opening in your heart and mind, and to allow I AM I AM to be reflected in and through you, without distortion. You have the opportunity to recreate yourselves and your world in perfect harmony.

I wait, and try to reach out to you more directly and emphatically from time to time. This is one of those times. You are on the brink of a new age that will be very different. It is important that you learn who you are, and what your creative power really is, and what your power has caused, and what consequences are likely if you do not begin to turn things around significantly, and soon.

I say I AM all that you create, and a great deal More. Some thinkers have posed theories that you created God, motivated by fear in a dark and dangerous world, or by loneliness in a cold and harsh existence, or by a sense of inadequacy that begs the presence of a higher being. Actually, over your entire history, you have created quite a spectrum of notions about God, some of which have become belief systems that breed hatred, war and other abuses of the human spirit and of this earth.

You have created all these various thought patterns, and I AM your creations because I AM All That Is. However, regardless of all that you have created, I AM still the I AM that I really AM, and so are you.

6. I AM Your Imagination

Thoughts are things. All of creation is thought — mine and yours. Thoughts are real vibrations, real energy in the world. You have learned, at least in some schools of thought, that there is real value in visualizing — picturing goals as already accomplished. You think those thoughts and send those pictures into the atmosphere. Your thoughts project real vibrations into the world, and they seek vibrations of like frequency, compatible with accomplishing the pictured goal. And it works. Many have achieved goals by concentrating their attention on pictures they paint in their minds. Most inventions are born in the imagination. Most crimes, too.

Think about the world you know, and all the dark, hateful, hurtful thought forms that exist in a given moment, and then multiply it millions of times, over millions of centuries. Can you imagine how many of those energies have been projected into the atmosphere here? I AM your thoughts and your imagination. I AM the pictures you paint, whether they reflect Light and Love or separateness and fear. Can you imagine what it's like to be that dark cloud of your fear?

You will enjoy life a great deal more if you allow me to be the I AM that I really AM in each of you and in all of creation. This does not mean you should relinquish your creativity or your individuality. You are not designed to be robots. I could have saved a lot of trouble if that was all I wished to manifest. I've done that before, and those worlds still exist, and I love them always. But you are different. You have the ability to create thought forms. You have imagination. I AM All That Is, and I AM your imagination. I love your imagination, but I do not always enjoy being the energy that flows there, or the consequences of that energy.

7. I AM Your Thoughts and Deeds

You are free to be the I AM that I AM, or to imagine, think and do your thing under the cloudy illusion of separateness.

Your thoughts determine your deeds. Like your imagination, your thoughts and deeds are real energies, having real impact in the world. You are so much More than you think. Your power can build or destroy this world, and you exercise much of this power unconsciously.

It is vital that you understand this power. That you learn who you are in this world, and unlearn the misconceptions you have inherited about who and what you are, who and what I AM, and who and what all of creation is. So you can more easily choose to love yourself, to love your neighbor as yourself, to love your world and everything and everyone in it. Knowing who you are and what power you have will encourage you more and more to open your left side to God's presence in your right side, and to allow the Energies of Light and Love to flood your consciousness, and your whole being.

I AM Great Mystery, Great Spirit, All That Is. I AM the Image and Likeness. The world and all its inhabitants. Humankind, right side and left. I AM your creations — your imagination, your thoughts and deeds. You have the ability to reflect whatever image and likeness you choose, and you are responsible for what you reflect. It is a heavy responsibility, especially now in these rapidly changing times. Your choices will beget consequences. You can turn this world around with Love. Individually and collectively, you can release fear and all its offspring from your energy field. Collectively, when enough of you are allowing Light and Love to be the Energy that radiates through your imagination and your thoughts and deeds, you will literally release fear and negativity from the earth plane. You can release or transmute all energies that generate destructive consequences.

I cannot overemphasize that you will always retain your individuality. You will enhance your personality, your humor and your talents, as you learn to know, love and access the awesome power of your Oneness, as you step into your particular role in these momentous times.

CHAPTER THREE: I AM HUMANKIND

1. I AM Your Free Will

Your free will is a thought form I expressed. And regardless of how you use it, your free will is a thought form that I AM.

In all of creation, free will is unique to humankind. Deep inside, you are still the I AM that I AM as you. You are still One with God and with all of creation. But for a very long time, most of you have not enjoyed conscious awareness of that Oneness. In all of creation, only humankind have the option to shut out your Real awareness by imagining a stage play and so immersing yourself in it that the play consumes your conscious attention.

The illusion of separateness takes many forms.

I have eternity to wait for you to come around, to wait for you to remember. To wait for you to allow yourselves to vibrate only at the higher frequencies where you realize your Oneness with All That Is. You also have eternity to come around to that realization. You do not, however, have eternity here on earth to achieve this level of being. You need to awaken to the More that you are, and to the More that your free will is. This is a time of epoch transition.

You are the 'Last Call' generations of manwomankind on earth. These days, all your free will choices will ultimately boil down to this: You will choose to open your consciousness to the higher energies of Light and Love, and to allow your consciousness and your whole being to be flushed with God's Energies and raised to a higher level of awareness with your Earth Mother, or you will choose to stay in the grip of fear's vibration and lose your opportunity to achieve those higher levels here on this planet.

You freely created your environment, including the clouds of illusion throughout the earth plane that give you amnesia when you incarnate here. You freely chose to be the ones here now, to be the ones to penetrate and dissolve those clouds from inside the Garden. You freely chose to be responsible for manwomankind's future on earth. To come here again, with no guarantee that you would choose to reawaken.

I cannot force you to believe any of this. I can't force you to alter your perspectives. Can't force you to open the door from your left side to allow the Me of you to flow through your whole being. Can't force you to allow All That Is into your consciousness. Can't force you to learn or unlearn what you need to learn and unlearn. Can't force you to remember who you are. Can't force you to stop killing each other, or to stop killing your Cetacean friends. Can't force you to stop destroying so many of the Earth Family's other life forms.

I AM your free will, but you control and exercise it. Even if I control and direct all the situations, circumstances and conditions around you, I cannot force your response to them. I do in fact control and direct much of what you each encounter, hoping always to present you with clues — stimuli to awaken you to my presence in and around you. But I can't force you to notice.

Open your heart and mind to the possibility that your free will can assist you and everyone around you in finding your way out from under that cloud of illusion. You can freely choose to open your physical consciousness to the energies of Unlimited and Unconditional Love, and to allow the Love that I AM to fill your being and radiate through you into the physical plane all around you. You can freely choose to allow yourself to become who you really are, individually and collectively.

2. I AM Your Path

Just as I AM whatever Real or unreal reality you choose to create, I AM also whatever path you choose to walk. I AM the One Real Path for all of creation, and I AM every path you choose within the framework of illusion.

Your frame of reference and your path have been restricted, much like Foot's. You are so much More than you realize, and there's a so much More to the 'Whole Truth' of creation than your current framework of physical consciousness can grasp. Together, however, we can substantially broaden that framework.

Has not each and every one of you, at some time in your life, felt a deep sense of loneliness, a longing for Something More? Loneliness is a trademark of paths in the illusion of separateness. For ages you have been creating these lonely paths that so many of you walk today. I know. I walk them there with you, in you, through you.

The True Path is the I AM that I AM, right there within you, at the edge of your consciousness.

Eons of humankind's choices have created the illusory path of separateness, and all its fear and loneliness. Countless generations of experience on that path have produced thick walls of definitions between your consciousness and your Oneness.

Thick walls between your right side and your left. Walls between your present self-image and your real possibilities. Like the wall between Foot's consciousness and its whole self.

I AM All That Is. I AM your illusions of separateness, your loneliness, and all those thick walls. I AM the path you have created. I AM also your Real Possibilities. I AM the Path back to the Oneness you truly are.

Constructive use of your free will can break down those thick walls, and dismantle the framework of definitions that so limit the path you walk. You don't have to do the dismantling yourselves. You need only choose to open even a small door in the direction of your right side, and to consciously allow God to help you break down those walls and limitations forever. You need only choose to allow God to help you back to the Path I Really AM.

You can walk the path of unreal reality for many more miles and many more ages, or you can choose to open your consciousness to the energies of who you really are. You can choose to allow your misconceptions to melt away. To allow your walls of separation and loneliness to dissolve. To walk the One Path that I AM.

It is not a journey of distance. It's a journey from the dimension of your freely chosen and inherited path of illusion, to the dimension of the I AM that I

AM as your Real Path. To the dimension of the Real Reality that you are — Light, Love and Energy or Life Itself.

It is Mother Earth's journey, the journey of your solar system, the journey of Light and Love in physical expression, and the journey of all human spirits who choose to participate. I AM the Path. Yours is the choice.

3. I AM Your Illusions

It will become vital that you begin to understand the I AM that I AM. It will become vital for you to realize that I AM your free will, and all your choices, creations and consequences. I AM the paths you create and walk, and all the illusions you have generated, accumulated, and inherited, throughout all time. The whole cloud.

I AM the Source. All-Powerful, All-Knowing, All-Present, and More. However, I cannot dispel your illusions by force. I respect your free will, regardless of what consequences your illusions might cause. I have tried many times in many ways to convince you of one thing or another, but I have never forced your will.

I will not prevent your freely chosen illusions from running their course. They've caused great destruction in the past. The history you do know sufficiently demonstrates that you've carried some detrimental patterns through one civilization after another. You must know how damaging it is to hate, to make war, to hoard, and to abuse. And yet these realities continue. As a race of beings, as a human family, you have left a great deal of debris in your path. You know this is true. You don't need me to tell you that some patterns of your history beg not to be repeated.

You've made progress, too. You've expanded your knowledge and developed your ability to survive comfortably in this world, though that will change. You've retained and honored much from Jesus, Mohammed, Buddha and others who've tried to show you a better way. Despite the cloud of illusion, you've still retained some Truth in consciousness. Hopefully it is enough. Enough to assist you now at this crucial time in your history and Mother Earth's, when you will either face the Reality about your illusions or face the reality of their consequences.

These are not threats. I only hope to help you see that your belief systems have largely been conceived in the illusory framework of separateness. The momentums of these unreal realities invite consequences you don't really need, won't like, and can avoid, by rising above them. I only hope to convince you that you are More than most of you yet think. I hope to convince you that I want you to have the opportunity to continue advancing here with and as part of Mother Earth, so you won't have to start the whole process over again, of developing a high frequency instrument in the physical plane that can eventually combine physical and spiritual consciousness successfully.

My Love for you and in you is Unlimited and Unconditional. I hope to convince all of you, if possible, to let your illusions go, to open to the

Presence that I AM in each of you, and to allow my Light, Love and Energy to transform and awaken you, as Mother Earth is transforming and awakening.

I would prefer not to be your illusions or their consequences, but the choice is yours. Please choose to allow the I AM that I AM to dissolve your illusions and their consequences.

4. I AM Your Return to the Right

Now is the time to begin releasing whatever concepts block your path. As I said, you have retained some of the Truth you've received and discovered, and you have misunderstood much of it, too.

Here are some of the more significant truths you've retained: God is Creator and Source, and created humankind in God's own image and likeness, and as free will beings. Jesus is God, and is the Way, the Truth and the Light. God is Love and loves all of creation. God is the Source of all Life. The Source of all Light. The Source of all Love. God is I AM I AM. God is Everywhere. God wants you to love yourself, your neighbor, your earth, and your connection to All That Is.

There's More meaning in these few statements than you might yet realize. They represent what you have always known on your right side, since you first came into being. I AM Light, Love and Energy, or Life Itself, and so are you.

I AM All That Is. So are you, despite your insistence on seeing yourselves only as Feet lost in the Garden, separated in consciousness from All That Is. I AM your right side and your left. I AM your free will, your chosen path, your Real Path, your illusions and your Truth. I AM your choice to dispel the illusions, if you will but make that choice.

I AM your Return to the right.

If you freely choose to open your doors to my Light, Love and Energy, and allow, we will become the I AM that we truly can be as you, reflecting purely and radiantly the Light of Love you came here to be.

This return to the Right, this opening and allowing, this process of learning who you really are and how to become who you are, is just that — a process. It involves many steps, many choices, much learning and even more unlearning. It involves opening to the Possibility of More. It involves opening to God's Energies and allowing the flow through your being in whatever increments are appropriate for wherever you are in any given moment. Whatever your vibrational level can handle. One step at a time. Too much at once would overload your circuits.

Many of you have already seen some of the More that lay beyond the definitions you inherited. Many have already learned to allow Spirit into consciousness in one way or another, connecting with the kind of guidance that Foot might receive from your whole self, once you got Foot's attention. Some of you hold dearly to age-old belief systems because that is how you learned to sincerely love God. Some of you don't know what you believe, if anything. Some of you know you are lost, but not which way to turn.

Wherever you are, in any given moment, I AM there with you. You need only turn your conscious attention toward your God-Connection within, quiet your busy conscious mind, and allow. Wherever you are, any step you take toward your internal Right side is a step in the right direction.

Any new awareness you achieve or experience which helps you open to the Possibility of More represents a turning toward your Right side. A turn of the mind. A turn of perspective. A turn of the heart. A turn of momentum that triggers the flow of the I AM that I AM on your Right side into and through the rest of you, if you will but allow it.

5. I AM Your Struggle

Some of you hear the ring of Truth in the words and momentums here. Perhaps you feel joy, or perhaps a stirring of those deep-seated longings for Reunion. Some will recognize my words as feelings you've known but could not express. Some of you already know all these Truths and are glad to see them written in simple language. Some will feel as though a Light has suddenly been turned on inside. Some will feel the waves of the Love that I AM, coursing through these words and through your physical consciousness. Some will feel the Energy of Life whirling around within you a little more or a lot more than ever before. Some will see these words as a door appearing suddenly, where before you saw only a wall.

More of you, however, are likely to struggle with these words and ideas, because they seem to threaten treasured belief systems, and seem to threaten your image of who you are, what life is about and who God is. Many will see this book as an attack on the God you love. And for many of you, your love of God is as earnest and sincere as any love can be. You are especially likely to struggle with what I AM saying. This will be a greater struggle than some of you have ever before encountered.

Especially to those who say you believe in and

love God, and have committed yourselves to serving God, I say this: All things are Possible With God. I AM I AM, and I AM indeed your very struggle.

To all who might be inclined to reject what I'm saying because of your belief in God, I invite and encourage you to ask God to protect you from falsehood. Ask God for guidance. Ask God to help you open only to what God wills to move through you. And please, ask God to really help you to be open to God's Truth, wherever that may lead you. "Thy will be done...."

These Truths I share with you, and this Path I hope to lead you on, this return to the Right, will involve struggle to some degree for even the most open-minded of you. Even you whose hearts already sing with the promise of long-awaited reunion. Even you who have already allowed Spirit to dance in your consciousness.

There is much to learn, and much more to unlearn. You never know in advance what you need to unlearn, because it's part of your belief system. Your conscious awareness needs to expand, to stretch beyond current limits. Often a struggle, and sometimes a painful one, just as you sometimes experience pain while stretching a muscle in exercise, the very process that strengthens it.

The struggle will be more painful and frustrating for some than for others. Childbirth can be difficult or relatively smooth, but always there is some stretching and squeezing, some struggle, and then a complete transition for the newborn, into a whole new world, infinitely more expansive than the womb of gestation. The Universe is already in early stages of 'labor.' You and Mother Earth have already begun the struggle of personal and global upheavals caused by universal contractions, stripping away what cannot be taken into higher frequencies, and moving into positions more conducive to a successful transition through this birthing, into a radiant new world.

You will determine the degree of your struggle's difficulty. It will depend on your willingness to open your heart and mind — your physical consciousness — to the God Presence within and all around you. It will depend on the degree to which you will consciously allow God's Energies, God's Graces, to flow through your entire being.

What if some of your circuits, or your channels of communication, are part of that eighty-some percent of your brain you haven't been using for so long? Like someone scrambled your channels, and left you thinking your tuners could only receive low frequency signals on local stations.

Those unused circuits might be likened to a system of water pipes in a park that's been closed down and locked up for many years. The pipes are clogged with accumulated minerals, dirt and other dried-out debris. Let's say you want to reopen the park. Hoping to flush the plumbing with fresh water, you open the main valve. But the clogged pipes don't allow the water to flow, and nothing comes out at the faucets. Yet, if you leave the valve open, the water will eventually work a path of moisture through the debris, until finally you see the first muddy drops at the faucet. Soon the drops turn into a trickle, then a small flow, always flushing out a little more debris, and then a little more, steadily increasing the pipes' capacity to carry that flow. The flow of water cleans the pipes and then uses their instrumentality to carry and distribute that precious water wherever it is needed through the park.

When you sit down and purposely attempt to open your consciousness to your God Presence, you may be opening valves to some of those clogged pipes. Just keep allowing. I will work that path of moisture through your consciousness. Don't get discouraged while you're waiting for those first drops at the faucet of your conscious awareness. And don't forget, the first drops might well be muddy — a little confusing. The more you allow, the more the flow increases. The more the flow increases, the more your pipes and circuits are cleansed and reactivated, and the more your frequency rises and your capacity to allow continues to expand.

I AM all of Creation. All of Humankind. I AM

your free will and the path you choose, Real or unreal. The illusions you create and those you have inherited. I AM your Return to the Right, to Truth, to Oneness. And I AM the struggle that you all experience in this process of learning and unlearning, this process of your Return to the I AM that I AM as you.

Ask for God's help. I will not let you down, however difficult your personal struggle may be. If you sincerely ask for God's help and open yourself to God's Light, Love and Energy, your struggle will not be nearly as difficult as it may seem to you now. I would much rather be your struggle than your illusions or their consequences, especially when you are struggling toward the Truth that I AM. Seek and ye shall find. If you are seeking Truth, you shall ultimately find the I AM that I AM in you and in all. You shall find One Light, One Love, One Energy. You shall find a whole body where you thought there was only a Foot.

It's worth the struggle.

6. I AM Your Victory and Your Defeat

I AM All That Is, and so are you. There is no concept in this book or in all of creation that is more important for you to remember, for you to accept down in the core of your being, than the concept that I AM All That Is and so are you. Accepting or rejecting this Reality will determine your victory or your defeat in this world.

I wish to be your Victory. Your success. If you do not succeed in making the vibrational transitions necessary to survive on earth, then I will be your defeat. Not my preference, but not my choice to make, either.

Always when you've broken this Earth and rubbed out her civilizations, it's been the result of free will choices made in the framework of separation. Your thoughts, choices and actions do spark momentums of energies that exist as part of the earth plane. Momentums accumulate. They can and do erupt as cataclysmic destruction.

The surface of the earth has been all ocean, all land, all ice, all cloud. The continents and seas have been in all different configurations all over the globe. Poles have shifted, sometimes dramatically.

Advanced civilizations have come and gone, as have countless species of plants and animals . There are bright moments in your history, and there are dark momentums of fear and its children, energies that accumulate like storm clouds until they burst. Many victories, many defeats.

You have started over many times here. Sometimes you have destroyed yourselves and all that you had built, and sometimes I have sent energies to cleanse the Earth and her atmosphere in one way or another, to give the few that remained a fresh start on this Garden project. You know the story of the Great Flood, and a few ice ages. A drop in the bucket of fresh starts here on earth.

Often enough, the need for fresh starts represented your defeats — your failures to move forward as a group, as a civilization, as a culture, as a family. All of your defeats have been either self-inflicted, as in the case of high-tech war, or self-initiated, as in unleashing forces you can't control, like a good bit of the waste that now lies buried in so many pockets of Mother Earth's surface, or the accumulating effect of undersea and underground nuclear explosions.

I AM your defeats, and I AM the destructive forces you unleash. I take no pleasure being these unreal realities. No pleasure watching the Reflection distort. No pleasure being the twisted Image that becomes your self-destruction.

On the other hand, I AM also your Victories. Some civilizations of humankind on earth have made amazing strides toward becoming One with All That Is. Some have even succeeded.

Many have generated technologies far beyond yours. Usually, enough of humankind was lost in separateness and fear that those technologies were used destructively. Each time, humankind had created a fork in the road, and usually took the path booby-trapped with consequences of your illusions, which only led you farther away from your identity and purpose, from your real Truth, from your conscious connection with All That Is — your only Real Victory.

7. I AM Your Survival

I AM all of creation. All Real Reality and all unreal reality. Real Reality will last forever. Unreal reality will not. Real Reality is the I AM that I Really AM — Light, Love and Life Itself. The Real Reflection, the Real Image and Likeness, the Real Oneness, vibrating with the one pulse of All That Is.

I say again, this does NOT mean you are to sacrifice your individuality. Look around you. There are no limits to the variety in my manifestations and reflections, and you have seen only a small portion of them. You are the greatest of all my expressions. Your individuality, unique perspectives and variety of expression are part of your greatness, and have made possible so much of your art, music, invention and philosophy, here in this world you know and in worlds that have existed here before.

Remnants of civilizations unknown to you still lie hidden, waiting to be unearthed. They represent part of your history here, though not recorded in any of the sacred or secular records that have been available in these times. You will discover some of them soon. Some of you will see them and remember.

Given the context of where you are at this point in the history of this world, of this universe, and of all creation, it is important for you to know that I AM, and that I AM More available to your consciousness now than in a very long time. This is because the overall frequencies of the earth plane have been stepped up. Because the whole physical plane really is gearing up for a leap into a higher vibrational range of existence. Your frequencies will continue to accelerate along with Mother Earth's. But you have the power and the right to respond to these higher vibrations however you choose. While you're choosing, it could be very helpful to know who you are.

I AM the Way, the Truth, and the Light. I AM All That Is, All That Ever Was and All That Ever Will Be. I AM Light, Love and Energy. Your Real Self is my image and likeness. Beyond the cloud of illusion, you are the I AM that I AM. Distorted images will not be compatible with the vibrational range of the new cycle that approaches.

I AM the Only Way, the Only Truth, the Only Light. I AM your Survival, if you will allow me to awaken you from within. Allow me to be the momentum that enables your Victory.

You are completing a 26,000 year orbit around the Milky Way Galaxy, and beginning a new one. The cycle's path crosses over a point of beginning. You might compare it to a multi-tiered board game. When you go all the way around the board and back to 'Start' on the first level, you climb up and continue your game's journey on the next higher level. The momentums of your evolution, and the time-tables of Earth's Awakening were planned for this moment in time. The train you're on is fast approaching a track switch to another dimension. To a new level of earth plane existence. "All aboard that's staying aboard."

I hope to get you thinking a bit More about whether you really want to continue here on earth or not. You will only survive here in physical consciousness if you have assimilated the higher frequencies of Light and Love into your being.

The cloud of illusion which represents your book of inherited definitions vibrates at frequencies that will not hold together when the earth plane train switches tracks.

There is no 'doom and gloom' intended here. This is a joyous time. I AM anxious to see as many as possible make the leap with Mother Earth into a dimension of higher consciousness, where fear's lower frequencies won't be part of the framework. The whole universe looks on with anticipation. Your whole history with earth has been the gestation period, and the dawning of this new age triggers the birth of a global, planetary consciousness in which you will share if you remain.

Imagine you are out hiking, and you encounter a stream. It's too wide to simply step across, but not so wide that you couldn't jump to the other side, with a running start. You know you can't continue at the same pace and stride if you want to make the leap successfully. You have to change your stride and build up your momentum to make that leap across to the other side. If the opposite bank is elevated at all, you have to alter your approach even more. You gear up your energy and concentrate your focus. You might even have to leave some baggage behind.

There's no doom and gloom in the adventure of your leap across the streambed unless you choose to see it that way. Doom and gloom might apply if you stood at the edge of the bank watching others leap across, but were too frozen with fear to make the leap yourself. Doom and gloom would apply if you knew your side of the streambed would soon be crumbling, and that getting across represented your only survival, and you still stood frozen in fear. No doom and gloom in the leap across to the other side.

No doom and gloom in your leap to a higher dimension of consciousness. Only in the illusions that could prevent you from making the leap, that could prevent your survival here on earth.

As the earth plane moves toward higher planes of existence and awareness, the vibrational frequency of everything and everyone in the physical plane is being geared up, or 'quickened.' As free will beings, you can choose to open yourself to this quickening, to facilitate the process, to facilitate your awakening, and to facilitate the dissolving of whatever distracts you from remembering who you really are.

Those who live in climates where the seasons express themselves more severely are quite aware of the consequences of not adjusting to those changing seasons, or of not preparing for them. The universe is changing seasons, so to speak. You will need to begin adjusting, to prepare for the changes, so you will be able to withstand them.

This is not a threat, any more than a winter storm forecast is a threat. The storm itself could be threatening, if it caught you unprepared, but the forecast gives you the opportunity to gear up. It's an announcement, a word of caution, an invitation.

I'm telling you that a storm approaches. A flashing whirlwind of higher frequencies. If you are not already doing so, you need to begin turning your conscious attention to the higher frequencies within your being. You need to allow the higher frequencies that I AM to flush out your extra baggage — your illusions of separateness — and to help you release those fears, attitudes and definitions that weigh you down.

If you are willing to open to the Highest that is within you, and to allow the Light, Love and Energy that I AM to enter and permeate your physical consciousness, you will weather and appreciate the storm, and you will make the leap.

The Survival that I AM is right there within you. Please allow me to reactivate your conscious connection with God.

CHAPTER FOUR:
I AM THE WAY, THE TRUTH AND THE LIGHT

1.   I AM the One Way

I AM the Way, the Truth and the Light. Jesus spoke these words before he left the physical plane. Contrary to what many believe, Jesus was an ordinary man in all the same ways that you are ordinary men and women. At the same time, he was also divine.

And so are you.

Like Jesus, you are both human and divine. Physical and spiritual. You are here in this world and you are One with All That Is. Jesus learned to allow his God Presence to radiate through all aspects of his being. He learned to allow the I AM that I AM to purely and completely be the I AM that I AM as Jesus. He became in physical consciousness what all of you are in Reality — One with God and with all of creation. He realized and was keenly aware of his Oneness with all of you. "Whatever you do unto the least of these my brethren, you do unto me."

Many of you believe he was already God when he came here. He was, and so are you. So is all of creation. But for most of you, this knowledge has been separated from your conscious awareness, and therefore from your belief systems. Yet, you do have a choice. Like Jesus, you are free will beings. He had to choose, and he chose to allow God to be God in and through the instrument Jesus came here to be. There was no guarantee that the cloud of illusion in the Garden would not distract his conscious attention. No guarantee that he would remember who he is and why he came here.

Jesus was called. He was pushed and guided. His left side trained by his Right, over a period of years. Most of his life is not recorded in the Bible. He learned to open himself more and more fully to God's Presence, and to completely allow God's Energies to flow through him. He learned to allow his God Self to direct his purpose and all his movements.

He came to show you the Way. He showed you complete surrender of his will to God's. Complete surrender of his left side to the God Presence on his right. He showed you that the I AM that I really AM could shine through and as both sides. And remember, he said that you would do "greater things than these."

He showed you how to Love. He showed you how to pray: **"Thy will be done...."**

Jesus is all you think and More. And so are you, if you will but open your doors and allow the energies of your whole self to flush out the debris of illusions that separate your consciousness from knowing who you are and why you are here.

When Jesus allowed me to fully and completely be the I AM that I AM as Jesus, he did not become someone else. He did not lose his individual personality and traits. Did not lose his sense of humor or his love for his friends. He didn't become a 'God-robot'. He only became, in physical consciousness, who he really is. He became consciously One with God and with all of creation.

He told you that the most important law of life is to love God and love your neighbor as yourself. He asked you to remember him and to follow his example. He told you he'd given you enough to digest, and that there was much More to teach you. He said the Spirit of Truth would follow and be with you always, though most of the world would not see or recognize it. He told you the Spirit of Truth would guide you into full truth and would announce to you the things that are to come. Pentecost Sunday's events only began to fulfill that prophecy, when Spirit visited the apostles and disciples with a dose of instant enlightenment. Remember, they were gathered in fear. They were lost without Jesus to lead them. The Spirit I AM did enter their beings that day, to give them courage to teach what Jesus taught them, and to give them the ability to communicate with all who would listen, regardless of language barriers, and to give them greater understanding of what Jesus had taught, and what his life meant, and how they should proceed in following his path.

Manwomankind was simply not ready two thousand years ago to receive and assimilate the full Truth Jesus referenced. Some might not be ready yet, but time is running short.

Many of you have already learned a great deal more about your real identities, and many more are ready to learn. You all have the option, and only you can make the decision to open and allow.

This is not about professing belief in all the New Age stuff that in recent years has inundated your world. You don't have to accept this business about channeling, or talking with spirits. You don't have to believe that there will continue to be more and more energies and entities from all over the universe focused here, raising the overall frequency of this earth plane.

You don't have to believe that I AM I AM writes this book through Charbern. Maybe you believe Charbern made it all up. You don't have to believe anything, and I ask you not to take my word for it, unless it rings true when you sincerely go within.

What I do hope you will believe is that God is Love. That God loves you and wants to Love the world through you.

Most Christian religions teach that your purpose in life is to know, love and serve God. What does that mean?

Most of what you 'know' is what you have learned. Learning requires openness. You were taught the earth-mind framework and the book of definitions as soon as you entered this world, through your early years and your education. You were open to what you were learning, because you trusted those teaching you, because they were your parents or figures of religious authority. The process is almost automatic. One generation after another, passing down the collective consciousness that was created within the illusion of separateness, and it becomes your frame of reference, your understanding of reality.

You have unlearned some of the illusions, and now it's time to learn and know More of your Truth. God is directly available to you right there in your consciousness. If you can open to that possibility, then you can learn to access your God Connection, and to allow God to activate your circuitries, and to fill you, incrementally, with the Knowing that is the Way.

To 'love' is to allow the Light of Love that is Life to fill you up and spill over in all directions. I AM Love, and so are you. Be yourself. You can become, in your physical consciousness, Unlimited and Unconditional Love in action, in expression, in all that you create. Will you allow it to be so?

To 'serve' simply means to do God's Will. A real puzzle for many of you. You have associated God's Will with the Ten Commandments, and with the summary commandment Jesus gave you. The Ten Commandments were presented to humanity mostly as statements in the negative: Thou shalt **not** kill. Destructive, divisive behavior needed to be exposed, defined and limited, to help you learn to live together on this earth, to guide humankind on earth through the ages of Law and Judgment, and to set the stage for Jesus to introduce the Age of Love. He demonstrated Unlimited and Unconditional Love, and appropriately reduced all Law to One Law — the Law of Love.

To serve is to know and feel the intent of I AM pulsing through All That Is, and to willingly participate in the continuous flow of Light, Love and Energy, as Spirit guides and directs you. "Thy will be done." This is the true meaning of service to God: surrendering your whole self to God, who is Present within and as every fiber of your being.

You really can know God. You really can be a flow of Love in the world. That **is** your service, here and everywhere. God's Will is the Plan for all of creation to be consciously One with Love, reverberating and expanding in and through all the variety you can possibly create.

To serve God is to open your minds and hearts to your God Presence and to allow the flow of whatever God wills.

All these energies coming to earth from all over the universe, all this channelled input of higher frequency momentums, all the energy that moves through those instruments who have already awakened, all the energy connected with the movement of the solar system — this is all really happening. It's been happening for decades, with increasing intensity, as each member of the orchestra joins in at the appointed time. You have been bombarded with higher frequency energies that are changing you and your world on a cellular level. Your frequency is being raised. Turned up a little at a time, like a light with a dimmer switch. The more the frequency is raised, the more easily you can access Spirit in consciousness. It's always been available and possible. But now, in these particular times of transformation, conscious access to your own I AM connection is easier to accomplish than it was even a few years ago. The higher frequencies are breaking down the veil, dissolving the cloud, little by little, in these pre-dawn hours before the advent of new times.

I AM all these energies. I AM the higher frequencies. I AM the Way to knowing, and I AM the Knowing itself. The Way to Love, and the Love itself. The Way to Serving, and the Serving itself.

I showed you the Way through Jesus, and through many others. Many different paths to the mountaintop, but only One Way. I AM the Way, and I AM with you always.

2. I AM the One Truth

Regardless of all the definitions you have created
and inherited, there is One Truth. I AM Truth. Jesus
allowed me to move fully through his being, allowed
me to be the whole Jesus that I AM, and to be the
One Truth that I AM.

I've said your religions and philosophies have
preserved some Truth, and that you have also
misunderstood much of it. I mean no offense to
anyone, but the illusion of separateness has been a
powerful force for a very long time in forming the
foundation for your perception of reality and for your
belief systems. Much of that foundation is not Truth.

The Truth is, I AM I AM. All That Is. The Truth
is, all of creation reflects the I AM that I AM, or distorts
the reflection. The Truth is, I AM Light, Love and
Energy. I AM also all the distortions of Light, Love
and Energy that you have created and inherited —
the clouds of fear and darkness that cause you to
wage war against each other, against this Earth, and
against yourselves, and often in the name of God.

The Truth is, the beginning of a new age in a
new solar cycle is upon you. Your survival for much
longer here on earth will require withstanding higher
frequency vibrations than you have ever known. I
AM the Highest vibrational frequency — the Pure
Light of Love. The Truth is, your frequency needs to

rise and your field of awareness needs to expand beyond your physical senses.

The Truth is, you know this, but you have forgotten.

I AM the Truth. Allow me to be your Truth, and I will help you remember.

3. I AM the One Light

There is only One Light. All of Life and all of creation is that Light, in an infinite variety of expressions and frequencies. I AM Light, and so are you.

Jesus told you, "Do not hide your light under a bushel basket." The bushel basket hiding your light is the shroud of fear, the cloud of illusion, and self-imposed limitations. The bushel basket is anything and everything that obscures the true radiance of your Light. The basket hides your Light from the world, and from your own consciousness as well.

Many of you have prayed for help to spread God's Light and Love in the world. A simple, beautiful, and effective prayer. By all means, ask for God's Light. Ask God also to help you open to God's Light, and to help you to allow that Light to awaken and activate you. You really are able to consciously permit God's Light to enter your energy field and shake loose the bindings of those baskets you've been weaving. Ask God to help you see the Light. Open your mind and heart consciously to God's Light. Allow God's Light to penetrate even the deepest and darkest corners of who you think you are.

I AM the Way, the Truth and the Light. If you will allow, I will Light your Way to the Truth.

4.   I AM the One

Some of you will struggle with much of this. Some will think I conveniently over-simplify. Some will feel threatened, though I threaten no one. Some will say I attack treasures of your belief systems, or of your religions, or even that I AM trying to lead you away from God.

I keep saying, don't take my word for it, or anyone's, unless it rings true in your heart and mind when you sincerely go within, seeking your connection to God. That's the point of it all, anyway — to know you have this Connection, and to access the direct Guidance you can allow God to be.

While I say "Don't take my word for it," I will say in the same breath that everything I AM writing here is true. I know some people will have trouble accepting that. To all who doubt the Truth of what I AM telling you here in this book and there within your being, I offer this suggestion:

There is only One God. Pray to the One God. Ask God to protect you from falsehood, and to shield you from those who would lead you away from God. Ask God to protect you from those who would in any way deceive you about the Way, the Truth and the Light. Ask God to

**deliver you from anything and
everything that is not truly God's
Way, God's Truth and God's Light.**

If you can say this prayer and mean it, and if you
do truly seek God's Way, Truth and Light, then you
must be willing to really open yourself.

**Ask God to help you to know the
Way and to know God as God wants
you to know God. Ask God to help
you to love God as God wants you
to love God. Ask God to help you to
serve God as God wants you to
serve God.**

Do you think I would encourage you to pray this
way if I were trying to lead you away from God? You
decide.

You've been working against yourselves here on
earth for a very long time. The Self that you really
are is so much More than the self most of you think
you are.

There is only One Self. I AM that Self, and so
are you.

Remember the analogy of the Foot? Getting
Foot's attention is only part of the process of
reconnecting. You also have to earn Foot's trust.

When you first pierce the veil at the ankle and shine a ray of communication that gets the foot's attention, it has no idea who or what you are. No way to confirm or deny the truth of what you say.

You look down at the big picture of Foot's surroundings and say, "Your very best next step is a hard right turn." Foot looks around and senses that a hard right turn is not in the direction of the destination, and says, "No way. I don't trust you. My destination lies straight ahead."

Foot has free will, so you bite your tongue and watch. Foot moves ahead and finds a deep ravine cutting off its path just over the first rise. Maybe then Foot looks back up to you and asks, "Which way did you say?"

I AM the One Way, the One Truth, the One Light, the One Self. Open your doors to the One that I AM, and allow. I AM the One. So are you....

5. I AM the Only One

As I have said, and have told you many times over the course of your history here, there is only One God. I AM the I AM that I AM. The One God, the Only God, in you and in all.

I AM available to each of you individually, wherever you are, when you choose to open to the possibility and allow my Presence in your physical consciousness.

6.   I AM the One Who Helps

I AM all the Help you need to return to awareness of who you are, and to awareness of your Oneness with All That Is.

If it is your purpose to know, love and serve God, I AM your Purpose and the Path to it, and I AM whatever Help you need to achieve your purpose. Allow me to Help you. Allow me to fill you with the Light of a higher vibration. Allow me to Help you remember. Allow me to help you become consciously aware of the world of Spirit all around you. Allow me to cleanse your minds and bodies of all that obstructs your path to Oneness. Allow me to heal your every illness, in mind and body. Allow me to Help you to know, love and serve the I AM that I AM in you and in all. I can do all these things and More, if you will but allow me to be the I AM that I truly AM in and through you.

I AM not telling you to give up your religions and organized prayer. Most religions are founded on loving God and neighbor. You do need to realize, though, that no church has a monopoly on the whole Truth. Religions and belief systems of many cultures have preserved a great deal of Truth, some of it common to many religions, and some specific to a few. What I AM telling all of you who say you believe in the One God is that I want you to know that One God, personally.

I AM far More than any of your belief systems can define. More than all of them. I AM the I AM that I AM regardless of definitions. Throughout your history I have given you various glimpses of the I AM that I AM, and you have understandably taken those glimpses and built altars for them and walls around them. Even Jesus. You put him on a pedestal, separating him, thereby excusing yourselves for not being able to follow his example. He told you, "These things and More...."

It's time for you to get More than a glimpse. It's time to rise above the clouds of illusion. Time to dismantle the baskets. Time to remember who you are. Time to reconnect in consciousness what has always been connected in Reality. I ask you, allow me to Help you see More.

I AM asking you to open your doors to the Whole Truth that I AM. No matter what religion or school of thought frames your belief system, I ask you to consider the Possibility that now there is More that God wills to share with you, because it is time. Pray for protection from falsehood, but pray also for Help in opening to whatever God's Will really is. Pray for Help in learning to allow the flow through your physical consciousness of whatever God really wills for you. Pray for Help in being open to whatever God's Help really is.

7. I AM the Help of All

I AM the Path to the Oneness of All. I AM everyone's Path. You really need to become more tolerant of each other's belief systems. You need to look more at what you all have in common rather than at what separates you. Nothing that is based in Real Reality can separate you. I AM the One God, the God of All. How many families do you know whose members are all exactly alike? Not too many, I would bet. Humankind is diverse, and yet you are all One Family. Your religions must accept this premise if they are to Help rather than hinder your progress toward becoming who you really are. A constructive family will set differences aside and focus instead on the love and common bonds they do share.

The Light that I AM is always available to all of you, regardless of your religion or lack of it. Accessing your connection will get easier as the earth plane frequency rises, and that much more so as your individual frequency rises.

An extremely high frequency, high intensity Flash of Light will officially mark the beginning of the New Age. Any who are open and have learned to dance with the new vibration will Light up with information and awareness. You need to gear up for this Flash. I can Help each of you in whatever way is needed.

I AM the God of All and the Help of All. The One God and the One Help. I AM the Only Help for Manwomankind on earth.

You have called me many different names and envisioned me as many different forces. I AM All of them and More. I AM the I AM that I AM, and I AM the One Path to the Oneness of All. I AM your individual Help. I AM your collective Help. I AM the Only Help — for you, your friends, your enemies — for All.

CHAPTER FIVE:
I AM THE LEARNING AND THE LEARNED

1. I AM Your Path

I AM your individual path and your collective path to the Oneness of All. I AM all your paths. It's not my preference to be many of the paths you have created, leading from one illusion to another, away from your Oneness, away from waking up to your true Self.

It's not my preference to be destructive paths you create with your waste and your abuse of natural rhythms and resources. Not my preference to be paths of fear and separation that weave the baskets that hide your Light.

It is my preference and my sincere hope that you will allow me to be your path to your Real Self, especially now when your continued existence here in this Garden is at stake. This Garden is preparing to leap to another dimension of existence, where it will remain and where it will thrive. All who are prepared to blend with the frequencies of the Fourth and Fifth Dimensions will also make that leap. You all have the potential to assimilate this transition that is upon you, and to make a successful leap. But the transition will intensify and escalate. When the new age really begins, a much brighter Light than you have ever seen or felt will inundate the earth plane. If you have not embraced the higher frequencies of Light and Love, you simply won't be able to withstand the vibration. Physically, emotionally, mentally and spiritually, you would be like fish out of water.

Again, this is neither threat nor punishment. It is simply the universe unfolding as it should, as it was designed. You are designed to be One with this unfolding, One with this Awakening, and you can be.

Whatever path you choose, I AM your Path. At any present moment, at every present moment, you can choose to open your individual door to the I AM that I AM. You can choose to allow my energies to flow through your physical consciousness. You can allow me to help you back to the One Path, and to help you in the process of becoming One with the Path that I AM.

You will never regret opening your inner door to the I AM that I AM, and you will never regret allowing my Light, Love and Energy to flow through the circuits of your being. You will never regret allowing me to be your One Path.

2. I AM Your Steps On the Path

I AM I AM in every present moment. I AM all the unreal realities you have created over eons of history. I would rather be your steps back to the path and your steps on the path — the thoughts and actions that move you closer to your awakening, closer to your Oneness with All That Is.

I can only be your steps on the path if you open the doors of your consciousness and allow the waves of my Energy to flow, at whatever rate is appropriate for you. Every time you consciously choose to open to God's Presence within you and allow, some level of cleansing and healing takes place, and your capacity to allow grows a little. Next time, you are able to open and allow a little more deeply, a little more fully, a little more broadly.

I can make suggestions. I can give you guidance. I can even beg. But I cannot force your steps any more than you could force the next step of your analogous friend Foot. You must choose, at every turn and in every present moment.

Choose to open your consciousness to the I AM that I AM in you and in all, and I will help you make those choices. I will help you to see and feel more clearly which choices will lead to the immeasurable joy of reunion with who you really are. I will help you with small decisions and large ones.

The more you open and allow, the more you become aware of my Presence, and the more you will find my Presence both comforting and energizing. I say, "Don't take my word for it," and in the same breath I guarantee that you will enjoy being on the Path that I truly AM, where your life-long search will end and your Real adventure will begin. You will enjoy remembering who you are. You will enjoy being the I AM that I AM as you.

Allow me to be the Steps on your Path.

3. I AM Your Steps Off the Path

You've created more steps off the Path than on it. Steps that don't reflect Light, Love and Energy. Not my preference to be those creations.

Again, I don't blame you for the illusions you inherit here, though you are connected, more than you might realize, to all that humankind has ever created anywhere. But here you are, in a cloud of misconceptions, your Light hidden from the world and from your own eyes by those baskets woven of separation and fear. You get amnesia when you incarnate here in the Garden. So, no, I don't blame you any more than the children who have fought so many of your wars are to blame for creating the circumstances that started them.

You are here now. You are the ones poised at the edge of this new age. You will determine how many will make the leap with Mother Earth to the Fifth Dimension.

When you step from a dark place into direct sunlight, your eyes hurt and struggle through tears to overcome the shock. If you can see at all, what you see is blurred. Much easier for your eyes to adjust to gradual increases in brightness, and to then encounter that direct sunlight with both comfort and vision.

The dawning of this new age will be like a million

sunrises. Intense, high frequency Light will saturate your solar system, vibrating you and your world to another whole range of frequencies, to another whole dimension of physical expression. Light waves vibrate in all frequencies. Higher frequency waves are shorter and vibrate faster than the longer, slower waves of lower frequencies. This Earth will soon be vibrating only the faster, shorter sine waves of Light's higher frequencies.

Your frequencies have already been quickened somewhat, and More of the higher energy is being channelled into the earth plane every day. The pre-dawn sky gradually turns from dark to light, ever brightening as the Sun prepares to explode over the horizon at its appointed moment. It's time to open your eyes and begin adjusting, if you haven't already, so you'll be able to stay and face the sunrise that will be like no other. Allow me to help you prepare for the brighter Light of a new awareness.

As always, you are free to choose. To accept me or not. To be One with the Path of All That Is, or to create more steps off the path, which will only bring you more bruises, bumps and dead ends, and will keep you from learning who you really are. Your steps off the Path keep you in a dark place under your basket.

During this time of transition, your steps off the Path prevent you from facing Light and adapting to the brightening sky. If you stay off the Path, you won't be prepared when the New Sun crests the horizon and melts down the lower frequencies that remain. Your steps off the Path will become your steps off this Earth. I AM your steps off the Path. I would much rather be your steps into higher consciousness.

4. I AM Your Teacher and Your Guide

There was a time when all of humankind was consciously aware that I AM All That Is, in potential and in manifestation. You are Spiritual beings having a physical experience, remember?

Many have spent a great deal of energy and conscious attention seeking God, or a deeper spiritual experience, or a higher purpose in life. By all means, continue the search. Seek and ye shall find.

It may feel sometimes like you're exploring uncharted territories. They are uncharted in your consciousness because you have forgotten. You have created and maintained clouds of confusion and thickly-woven baskets that keep you in the dark.

When your search ends, you will discover that all along you were finding your way back home, and back to Real Self Awareness. You will find God and your higher purpose. Then begins your real adventure.

You are like children who got lost in the woods, and stayed lost so long they eventually forgot they were lost. Forgot their home and family beyond the woods. They grew accustomed to the dimmer light in the woods, as though it was all Light could be.

Your woods is the book of definitions, written in the framework of the separateness illusion. Your woods is the basket that hides your Light. It's the Foot's perspective. Your woods is the thick cloud of fear and confusion, the lower vibrations that have mesmerized and captivated your consciousness, as though the whole 'you' were contained in the body you wear.

You do have a family beyond your woods. Millions and millions of brothers and sisters — human spirits. They watch you in your self-made darkness, and hope always for your return to awareness. They actively shine the Light, Love and Energy I AM into the woods of your earth plane, every day. Your Family of Light participates vigorously in this project Awakening Earth. I speak of those who never ventured into the illusion of separateness, and of those who did, but have since returned. I have been their Return to the Path and their Steps On the Path. I AM their Path and their Oneness. Now I AM the Teachers and Guides they have become for you. I AM the Light, Love and Energy that radiates through them now, into the woods where you dwell.

Some delegation of your Family of Light has always been with you. But never before have they gathered in such great numbers to focus and direct my Energies into the woods. Through them, my Light has inspired your Bible, Koran, Torah and other sacred writings you will find. They've expressed my Love to you through angels, mystics and prophets. They've inspired much of your art, invention, democracy and global consciousness.

Now, over the last twenty years or so, both their

presence and their work here have intensified. Before you came to this life, you knew you'd get amnesia once you got here. You knew there'd be no guarantee you'd awaken and remember who you are and what's going on in the universe and why you came here. Members of your Family promised they would do everything they could to help you awaken. That's what they are doing now.

Many of you have tuned into frequencies of Spirit. Many have learned to allow all sorts of channelled transmissions to move through you into the world, covering a wide array of information and subject matter. One thread that is common to most of them is that they wish to help you understand who you really are.

Let me say very clearly at this point that there are many levels, many dimensions, many frequency ranges on the other side of the veil. Above certain levels only Truth can vibrate. But there are levels or ranges in the dimension closest to you where some of your spirit brothers and sisters are lost in a woods of their own, or are still lost in your woods. Not every entity who communicates through a channeller should be trusted or believed. "Don't take anyone's word for it...."

There are those who espouse the darkness they have created in their illusion of separateness. They dwell in fear and use fear to manipulate whatever they can frighten. They are not interested in the success of Awakening Earth. They fear it, as they fear all of you who learn to allow Light and Love to be the Energy you radiate. They would like to mislead you.

There are also those who mean well, but who aren't in their highest frequencies yet, who may only be returning to the Path and may still need to learn the Path itself, may still need to allow their own frequencies to be raised. Some think they know more than they really do. Some transmit very helpful information and energy. Some will mislead you despite their good intentions, and some would still entangle you in their own harmless but self-important webs of illusion. The constructive purpose they all do serve is that they spread an awareness that there is Something More, beyond the veil.

As an example, let's say our friend Foot allowed its awareness to be expanded all the way up to the knee. This would be major progress for Foot, though still a long way from achieving the Big Picture perspective. With good intention, Foot turns to its friends to share its discoveries and to encourage them upward as well. While Foot will be sharing some of the real Truth about the More that exists, its message will still reflect significant limitations in perspective.

There are also many discarnate human personalities who aren't moving beyond the physical plane and can't seem to break their gaze from the familiar woods long enough to see the Real Light that calls them home. Some of these know little more than you do about who they are and where they are going. Some know far less than you do about anything. There is more variety on the other side of the veil than you see in the world around you.

I tell you solemnly, if you seek me you will find me. Please allow me to be your Teacher and your Guide from within.

Open the doors of your consciousness to God — to the One God who is All That Is — and you will find me there. You might not recognize me immediately, and most of you won't be able to see who or what moves those waves of Love through your being, so always ask for God's Circle of Protection, or surround yourself with Light and Love, every time you open the doors of your mind and heart. Ask God to help you open to only the energies that God wants you to encounter.

Sometimes you may need to be walked a little farther down some of your paths of unreal realities, to reach a vantage point from which you can see them more clearly. But if you open directly to God first, you will always be protected from being led away from the Path to your wholeness.

I AM I AM in all of you and in All That Is. I AM all the Teachers and Guides who are sending my Light, Love and Energy to you now. I encourage you to open your minds to God's Way, Truth and Light in whatever form God wants it to take. I encourage you to open to your own direct connection to God, and allow God's Light, Love and Energy to permeate your consciousness and your whole being.

I AM your Teacher and your Guide. I AM with you always. I AM your Deepest Inside. I AM Great Mystery, and Great Spirit Who Moves In All Things. I AM God-Goddess All That Is. I AM the I AM that I AM as each of you, and want nothing more now than for you to remember that. I hope you will open to my Graces, and allow me to raise the level of your conscious awareness. I hope you will allow me to guide you into that sunrise of sunrises.

I take all forms. As Teacher and Guide, you will find me Present in every moment if you will but open your hearts and minds to that Possibility. You will find me in your ancestors, so many of whom currently transmit my energies into the world on many different levels. You will find me in the Spirit Guides assigned to each of you for all or part of your incarnate life. You will find me Everywhere and Always if you will but open your hearts and minds and allow me to be your Teacher and your Guide, and allow me to help you learn and unlearn what you need to learn and unlearn, and allow me to help you become in physical consciousness the Masters of Light you are in Reality.

5.   I AM Your Learning

I AM All That Is. The truth and significance of this simple statement relates to everything I AM telling you on every page of this book, and to everything I AM telling you every day within your being. It relates to everything you experience and to everything you are.

Some of you might accept the assertion, "I AM All That Is," though its meaning remains for you somehow abstract and nebulose. You still think of me as something other than you, apart from you. Some of you visualize an image of God as 'in' everything or as everything around you, but not as the self that you are, not as the thoughts and experiences you have, or as the things you learn.

I AM Everything, not just Everything Else. I AM Everywhere, not just Everywhere Else.

It's a slight turn of the mind, a different perspective I hope to help you see. When you start to realize — not just learn, understand or accept, but realize — that I AM All That Is, you can more easily see the whole world around you in a different light. A different Light indeed — a brighter Light. A higher frequency, higher intensity Light. My Light. The Light that I AM.

Open your hearts and minds to God's Light, Love and Energy. Allow me to be the Learning that you require. None of you are beyond learning More. All of you need to learn More about who you are, who I AM, why you are here and what lies ahead.

Please open yourselves to the Learning that I AM, which will lead you to the Oneness that I AM, which will free you from the darkness of the woods, where you grew accustomed to the dimmer light, and where all your definitions have been framed.

Please allow the Real Learning that I AM to penetrate and permeate your being, to fill you with More and More of a sensing, More and More of a realization, that I truly AM present within you and all around you. More of a realization that I AM All That Is, including everything you are, everything you encounter, and everything you think and do.

Except in rare cases, Learning is an incremental process. But it can only happen if you consciously open to God and allow. Without some opening in the door of your free will, your left side won't have a clue of my Presence on your Right. The choice is always yours. But this time, your very survival here on earth is what's at stake.

6. I AM Your Unlearning

For many of you, Unlearning is more important than Learning. As long as you maintain the illusion of separateness and its book of definitions, as many still do, you aren't likely to accept any Learning that stretches or contradicts your belief systems. If you believe that the woods where you've been lost so long is the whole of your reality, you won't likely entertain the notion that this woods is like Foot's view of things and is only a particle of your Reality. This woods need not be the darkened place it has become.

If a child somehow learned wrong sounds for the letters of the alphabet, he/she wouldn't be able to read, write or speak the language properly. Might put the letters and sounds together in a way he/she understands, but wouldn't be able to communicate with those words in this society. You could try teaching the correct sounds, but the child will only Learn them if and when the child is willing to Unlearn the sounds he/she thought were correct.

It wasn't too long ago that anyone who thought the earth might be round was dubbed a fool. The book of definitions said it was flat — a 'truth' inherited and bequeathed by unsuspecting generations who had no frame of reference for doubting. A visionary proved that the inherited truth was wrong, and manwomankind unlearned it. The Earth is round. Many erroneous notions previously held dearly as truths have been proved wrong and have been unlearned. Some things are easy to unlearn, like the wrong directions someone may have given you to their home. Some things are more difficult to unlearn, like the belief that you are separate and apart from God. And one of Unlearning's greatest inconveniences is that you rarely know in advance what it is you need to unlearn.

Stay open to possibility. Maybe you are More than you thought. Maybe God is directly accessible within you. Maybe the proof is all around you.

As I said earlier, you will see proof that dolphins and whales are physical instruments of far More intelligence and far greater Love than you yet perceive. You will see proof of everything I have said, and some of the more publicized proofs will be helpful to those who are struggling.

The most important proof, however, is on the individual level. If you consciously open to the Highest that is within you and allow, gradually you will see and feel the proof that I AM Present within you, and perhaps you will then be More willing to expand the book of definitions about who you are and who I AM. The more you make the choice and perform the act of opening to God and allowing, the More you will begin to realize that you are indeed connected to God, that you are indeed connected to All That Is, and ultimately, that you are indeed the I AM that I AM as you.

Ask God to protect and guide you. Also ask God to help you to be willing to unlearn whatever you need to unlearn. I AM your Learning and your Unlearning. The Learning will come easy once you get the hang of allowing yourself to Unlearn, once you get the hang of allowing the Light, Love and Energy I AM to be the Spirit that moves you.

Don't you think Foot may have some erroneous ideas about what's up there past the ankle, that you will need to help it unlearn while you are trying to convince Foot who you are and who Foot really is?

Foot's illusion of separateness never did alter the Real Reality of its connection to the rest of you. Your illusion of separateness — your amnesia — never has altered the Real Reality of your connection to All That Is. The world was round regardless of belief in the unreal reality that it was flat.

The Light that I AM in most of you is still hidden, from you and from the world, under the unreal reality of your baskets. You can Unlearn the darkness that clouds your perceptions. You can release fear and all its offspring. You can choose to open and allow, and I will be the process of helping you dismantle the vary fabric of the basket. My Light will help you see the woods for what they are, and will help you see some of your 'truths' for the illusions they are. One by one, you will joyfully relinquish those beliefs that have for so long held you down.

I hope you will choose to unlearn what you need to unlearn, so you can become who you really are, so you can do what you came here to do. I remind you, the stakes are high this time. Mother Earth is undergoing major transitions. The earthquakes, volcanoes and storms of recent years are messengers of More to come. These are the days when the mighty Phoenix breaks through the surface and begins to shake off its wings, and the earth trembles. These are the days when you need to adjust to the higher frequencies of Light and Love. These are the days when you need to open your hearts and minds to Possibility. The days when you need to unlearn some wrong sounds for the alphabet of Life. When you need to have a conscious connection with Spirit.

Brighter Light and expanded consciousness will be the new substance and character of Mother Earth and of all those who leap with her into the Fifth Dimension. You are cordially invited to tune in to that Light and that Consciousness.

7. I AM Your Education

Education is a process. I AM that process. Your Education is my Light, Love and Energy. Your Education is the process of moving from where you stand in this moment to a higher plane, to greater awareness and understanding.

No teacher can truly educate a student unless the student is willing, to some extent, to open his or her mind and allow that education to take place. To allow is to permit, make room and listen.

Honestly, don't you think there could still be more mistaken impressions in your belief systems? Think of how many misconceptions you've unlearned in the past hundred years, regarding what is or is not possible. Some were beliefs etched in stone, though they had no foundation in Truth. Some limitations were valid for a time, until other inventions transformed them into possibilities. Like space travel, for instance.

Don't take my word for it, but you have not exhausted the list of misconceptions that cloud your perspective. You have much to learn and unlearn. You need More Education. You need to learn the alphabet of your Real language. The person with amnesia needs to learn about who he/she has been, and needs to see faces and places that were once familiar, in the hopes that something will trigger the whole memory's return.

You are so much More than you think you are.

Allow me to be your Education, from within you where I AM, and through so many of your Family of Light that I AM. They are the familiar faces and energies, and they hope to trigger your whole memory's return, as the day fast approaches when nothing less will do.

CHAPTER SIX: I AM YOUR FUTURE

1. I AM the Hope of Manwomankind on Earth

The Hope that I AM is the Real Hope for manwomankind. There is no hope for Foot to see the big picture until the Real you convinces it that More is possible. Until you convince Foot that it is part of you. Until you reconnect Foot's consciousness. In the analogy, you are the only hope for Foot. Just so, your only Real Hope to see and know the big picture is to allow your Real Self to reconnect your consciousness.

In the analogy, you and Foot can take your time if you want. The longer it takes, the more bumps and bruises Foot is likely to encounter; but Foot has free will and can take as long as it chooses.

In your Reality, there is more urgency. Oh yes, you have free will and can take as long as you want to explore who you really are. But you cannot take as long as you want here in this physical plane at this point in its history. There is a time limit here, set by the clockwork of the universe.

You are seeing major transitions throughout the world, and they accelerate. Changes in geography, changes in earth consciousness, changes in your bodies and your physical world on a cellular level.

When the new cycle begins, you will experience a different kind of 'physical'. A lighter physical. A higher frequency physical.

You only have a few of your years left to prepare. The events and changes are upon you now. It's time to wake up. I AM your Hope of awakening.

2.   I AM the Only Hope

The world as you know it is coming to an end. This is not a punishment. The reverse is true. You and Mother Earth approach a 'graduation' to the next level up, if you have the capacity to withstand and assimilate the higher frequencies there.

I don't threaten you with this wondrous transformation. I simply announce it, like the conductor on a train might call out, "Next stop: New Age and New Great Cycle. Only those with proper tickets may continue on this train now."

These things are on schedule and are going to happen, regardless of how many believe it, regardless of how many have the right ticket. If you choose to make the necessary arrangements and get your ticket in order, you stay on the train. And you will experience a more wondrous journey than you can even yet imagine.

If you don't have the right ticket, you get off the train. You don't get shot or beheaded or held up to ridicule. You just get off the train. You need to ride a train whose vibration is compatible with your ticket.

Remember, you are More than your body. You inhabit your body, blending your Spiritual nature to its physical one. At this time, the 'blend' is changing, gearing up to a higher power. Because of the interaction of Spirit in physical consciousness, the level of physical consciousness is being raised. If you are stuck on the old level and refuse to open yourself to this graduation, for whatever reason, you'll have to leave this earth and this life. The Real You will go on to other experiences, and your level of attainment in physical expression will determine how and where you will next incarnate, continuing your quest to blend Spirit in physical consciousness. You'll have to undergo the whole evolutionary process again, probably taking many more ages and eons to rise once again to where you are now, only to face again the same kind of choices that confront you here and now.

Now you have the opportunity to leap to another whole dimension of awareness, another level of blending Spirit and matter. Now you have the opportunity to evolve with Mother Earth, emerging with her as a single, throbbing Heart, perhaps eleven billion strong. A planetary consciousness reflecting only the Light, Love and Energy that I AM. This great leap forward is the long-awaited birth, and your entire existence on earth has been the gestation period. Your Real Hope is to go forward, not back. Your Only Hope of going forward is to awaken and participate consciously. I AM what you awaken to. I AM your Only Hope.

I know that many if not all of you will at some point, to some extent, struggle with issues of control and individuality as you explore this business of allowing. You do not sacrifice your individuality when you move toward your Oneness. You don't lose your capacity to create, to enjoy, to imagine, to laugh. You don't lose control over your life. You gain all these things. How much control does Foot have, despite what it might think? Doesn't Foot gain Real control when its consciousness is reconnected to its real brain?

Think about the children lost in the woods. When their Family finally does find them and shows them how much More there is beyond the woods, and shows them the way out of their dimness and into the brighter light of home, do you think those children are likely to lose their ability to laugh and think and be who they are? Or will they have a great deal More to laugh about, and to enjoy? They will have a much broader spectrum of awareness in which to think and imagine. And they will know the joy of reunion with their Real Family.

When they first got lost and couldn't find their way out of the woods, they could only hope they'd either find their way or their family would find them and take them home. They did not find their own way out, and were left only to hope. They stayed lost a long time. Meanwhile, acclimating to their surroundings, one generation after another, they eventually forgot they had family and forgot they were lost.

I AM your Family. I AM your Closest Relative, there within your very being. And I AM your whole Family of Light. I need to help you remember that you are part of the Family. As I said, the children in the woods might need to be exposed to sights and sensations of their real home and family to help them remember. Allow me to flush your energy field from within, with the Light of my Love, and some part of your consciousness will begin to remember that there is More.

You are More, and always have access to that More.

If you were the Family whose children were lost, you would search for them. You would find them and do whatever you could to help them remember, and to help them out of the woods that had become a wall around them. If you knew that the woods themselves were in danger, you would step up your activity to save your children. Their only hope is that you find them and they allow you to lead them out before the woods comes crumbling down upon and all around them.

Your woods is in danger. Jesus said his angels would remove all causes of sin — all the lower frequencies — at the close of the age. The cloud of illusion and all the definitions and destructive momentums that have been created in its framework will be dissolving. Whatever fabric remains of your baskets will disintegrate in the Light of the New Day. The lower frequencies will simply not be able to vibrate here. The higher frequencies will shatter them, as an opera singer's frequencies can shatter glass.

Like the children, it would be much better for you to watch the woods dissolve from outside them. Remember, I speak not of trees, but of analogous woods — the cloud of illusion and all its books of definitions. Their time has ended. They no longer serve any constructive purpose. They've been an integral part of the gestation period, but they are not to be part of the newborn in this time and place. They are not to be part of this Earth's life in the new cycle.

Your Only Hope is to emerge from the woods of illusion somehow, before they come crashing down. Your Only Hope of surviving the fall of the woods is to allow yourselves the chance to remember who you are. To allow yourselves to be shown a brighter Light. To allow the higher frequencies of your Real Self to vibrate you through this birth into a new dimension.

I AM the Brighter Light, the Higher Frequencies, the Path out of the woods. I AM your God Presence, and I AM your Only Hope.

3. I AM the Only Chance

It's difficult for some of you to hear these things without hearing them as threats. And you've had your share of sign wavers warning that the end is near and crying "Repent". You may be tempted to think this book and all the corroborating transmissions of Spirit all over the world are just a few new faces for the old doomsday syndrome. Just another fad. Of course, you can believe what you choose to believe. You can create whatever reality you like, and live with it. But Earth's upcoming Leap and Awakening is Real Reality, regardless of what anyone believes. Your belief will make a difference, though. It's a cause that will bring effect. Your belief will determine whether you will make the leap with Earth and your Family, or stay in the Third dimensional physical experience, beginning the whole evolutionary process, the whole gestation period, all over again, in some other place.

Any choice you make, any belief you create, any act you perform that's founded in the illusion of separateness — not consistent with the Light of Love that is Real Life — simply won't help you get out of the woods, and the woods of illusion in this earth plane are going to crumble. It's understandable that you might reject much of what I'm telling you. You've been lost in the woods for a long time. But please, stay open to Possibility. It's your Only Chance.

4. I AM the Last Chance

Your species is not the first group of humankind to get lost in woods of illusion here, nor the first to whom I have given this message about who you are and who I AM. You have become entrenched before in physical surroundings you created. You have watched the woods crumble before, and sometimes have crumbled with them. Many civilizations you know little or nothing about have come and gone. Many times you have devastated earth's balance, and your own.

Many times have you started over, developing awareness in physical consciousness, and trying to blend it with the higher frequencies of your Real Selves. Many times you have developed technologies that would make the present day seem primitive, just as your present technology makes that of fifty years ago seem primitive.

You've allowed yourselves to get lost in the woods before. Each time, you started over. Another chance.

It's different this time. This time is the Last Chance here on Earth. This world is going to change dramatically, bathing forever in a higher vibration, one that sustains an elevated physical state. When this new cycle begins, you will be crossing over the point where Earth came into being, and Earth begins a whole new level of existence, a new level of consciousness, and a new level of physical. This is the last time here for the physical you have known. You will become a Lighter physical. A more transparent physical. A physical that will require only thought to fashion. You will design and construct with imagination.

We'll get into more of that later. For now, what's important is that you begin to see that you might indeed be a little like the children who got lost in the woods, or like the Foot that lost contact with the rest of its Self. What's important now is that you begin to see that there is More beyond the book of definitions, that you begin to remember who you are, that you begin to open More to the Highest that is within you, and allow yourself to be flushed with the energies that will wash away illusion, and will awaken you to the More that you really are.

What's important now is that you realize that the Events and Changes are really upon you now, and will accelerate. That you begin to realize that you really can communicate consciously with your Real Family and with God, through your own direct connection. That you begin to develop your connection to greater awareness, so you will recognize the truth that this is indeed manwomankind's Last Chance on earth.

This earth has long been the central incarnating home of humankind. Now you have the opportunity to consciously evolve, with and as part of your home,

Mother Earth, in a quantum leap, to a level of existence that you will enjoy immensely if you choose to go along.

The lowest frequencies, the longest wave forms, like hatred, fear, greed, jealousy, bigotry and selfishness, will simply not be able to function in the range of frequencies where you will be doing your dance with Mother Earth. They will come apart, breaking down into universal substance which you will shape with your imaginations, into whatever reflections of Light and Love you can Energize.

You have the opportunity to graduate to Life in Greater Light, Greater Love and Greater Energy, where you will have greater awareness, greater abilities and greater adventures.

The opportunity is now — these next several years. Now is the time for you to open to the possibility that you might have something in common with Foot. To the possibility that God is I AM I AM, and is Present in you and in all, and is available to your consciousness. You have all the tools you need, and more help available than you could ever require. Literally, all you need to do is open the door of your conscious awareness to your God Presence, and allow.

5. I AM the Destruction

I AM your free will, and I AM your choices; but I cannot make your free will choices.

Many of your structures will crumble in earthquakes and storms as your Mother shifts into a new position, and many more will fall when she passes into her new cycle. Many physical structures and many thought pattern structures.

This crumbling, this dissolving into particles, will be part of earth's Magnificent Cleansing. It is not designed to be a negative destruction, as it might seem to many of you. You don't live in mud huts anymore. You evolved to far more sophisticated housing. The huts were long since swept away in the winds of changing times. You are here on this Earth at the time of her greatest change ever. You and Mother Earth are about to evolve to a more sophisticated form of physical consciousness, and you will have no use for baskets that hide your Light, as the butterfly has no use for its cocoon.

If you choose to remain in the woods, some sadness will be associated with the opportunity lost. I do not wish to be the Destruction of your opportunity on earth. I wish to be your Cleansing, as well as Earth's. I wish to accompany you on the adventure into the fifth dimension. I wish for all of you to become that successful blend of Spirit in physical consciousness, as you spiral into frequencies you previously thought were only science fiction.

It is always your choice. I ask you to choose Light and Love. To open your doors. To allow yourselves to become who you really are. To allow your Real Family to help you out of the woods. To allow the eyes 'way up here to guide the Foot 'way down there. I do not wish to be your destruction.

These are times that are predicted in the Bible, and in many other prophecies. These are not intended as times of destruction. These times are intended to be the end of the world as you have known it, the end of a world with hatred and war, and the beginning of the world in the brighter Light of Love.

6. I AM Your Survival On Earth

If you will open to God with real openness, and Learn to consciously allow the flow of God's Light, Love and Energy in and through your being, you will see the truth of all that I AM telling you.

Many of you pray for God's Grace. Ask God to help you to recognize and to really be open to that Grace.

When the time is appropriate, I will find ways to tell all of you if there is a need to evacuate your buildings and cities, if you are listening. I will show you the places that will be safe, where you will be able to watch and experience the wonder of passage into this new cycle. From within you and from within and as Mother Earth, I will teach you to rebuild and repaint the earth and your new world with the building blocks of your imagination.

I ask you to open and allow. I ask you to pray to God, whatever you call God, and whatever you conceive God to be, and to ask God to protect you from falsehood, and to help you to open to what God really wants for you. I ask you to allow me to be the Survival of humankind on earth, so you can continue as humankind on earth, and so you'll be able to make the great leap into consciousness. You will not regret it.

You are so much More than you have thought for so long. You are poised now at a time in history when you can correct all the mistakes humankind has ever made here, and you can do so from where you now stand, with your own personality, your upgraded consciousness, your lighter, healthier, more mobile physical body, and a very happy heart.

7. I AM the Alternative

I AM the choice you make, and want very much to be your choice for Light, Love and Energy, your choice to learn to become who you really are.

I AM Love. Love Itself. The Light of Love is Life Itself.

Love is the alternative.

Love is the real choice you must make in order to learn to make the leap. I said there would be no fear, hatred, greed or war. Only Love. Unlimited and Unconditional Love.

You've been struggling in the darkness of the woods, the darkness under the basket, the darkness within the cloud of illusion. Many of you have struggled courageously and beautifully. Allow me to be your Struggle, your Return, and your Awakening.

Choose Love and you will see Light.

The new cycle will begin with a great flash of Light Energy that you will see and feel if you have chosen Love — if you have opened to the Love that resides within you, and if you have allowed that Love to raise you up.

Ask God to help you open to God's Love, and to help you allow God's Love to fill you to overflowing. Ask God to help you to become who you really are — the Love that I really AM.

Choose the Real Alternative. Choose Love. Open to Love and allow. I will not disappoint you. One step or leap at a time, you will become, in consciousness, the Light beings of Love that you have always been in Reality.

CHAPTER SEVEN:
I AM YOUR ONE AND YOUR ONENESS

1.   I AM the Formula

I hope I've gotten your attention, and maybe I've broadened your perspective. I hope you'll consider the possibility that I just might be telling you the truth, that I just might really be trying to help you remember who you are.

I came into Charbern's consciousness through two of his Guides that I AM, who are of the same branch of the Vine that now expresses him. I had to stretch his belief system, convince him the communication was real, and earn his trust all at the same time. During that stage, he was understandably cautious, sometimes perplexed and frustrated, and sometimes not certain he should continue pursuing this process of conscious allowing. There was one proposition that kept him going. We told him, "If what we are telling you is true and you don't take us seriously, you stand to lose a great deal, and anyone who might have been helped through you also loses. If what we are telling you is a hoax, the worst that will happen is that you will make a fool of yourself, and you already know how to do that. Continue on, with a Wait and See attitude."

I say the same to all of you now. The stakes are high. You stand to win or lose the whole pot this time around. Take a 'Wait and See' approach, and stay open to Possibility.

I hope you now accept the possibility that there might be misconceptions in your book of definitions. That you might be More connected to the Gardener than you realized. That you might be more like those lost children than you may have thought.

I hope you now accept the possibility that I AM, both in this writing and there in your hearts and minds, trying to help you find your way out of the woods, trying to help you find your way home.

I briefly mentioned the Bible, the Torah and the Koran. What I say about the Bible is true for all of them, and for other writings as well.

The Bible was written only in the last few thousand years, and much of it was passed down orally for generations long before being written. Literal accuracy mingles with mystery, mistranslation and misunderstanding. Some stories and their significance were misunderstood long before they were written. The Word of God was received and recorded within the cultural frameworks of various times, within the cloud banks of the illusion of separateness.

The Bible is a Formula describing how to achieve your Oneness. Humankind was not ready to

understand or make use of the whole message, or
to see where it would ultimately take you. But you
could preserve its pieces.   It didn't need to be a
thick book to serve its purpose. Some stories were
added because they were meaningful to those telling
them. Even the New Testament, the least tarnished
by oral tradition, has been altered many times over
these past two thousand years.   Some
mistranslations relate to how it was copied for
preservation, and some misunderstandings relate to
cultural variations of translators who were influenced
by their values and by their particular edition of the
book of definitions. More numerous yet are the faulty
interpretations still being created by those who would
manipulate the word of God for their own purposes.

Further, there are aspects of Complete Truth that
are simply not spelled out in those writings.   The
Formula has always been there, and you have always
had access to it. The path out of the woods is always
available to you. But much of it was not spelled out
because you wouldn't have understood it until you
broadened your horizons and your frame of reference
again. I come to you where you are now. I came to
your ancestors where they were then. You can only
grow in present moments, in your now.

I'm not telling you to throw our your Bibles or other
sacred writings. On the contrary, I suggest you read
them, but with an open mind and heart. Ask God to

help you see the Bible through God's eyes. To help you recognize God's messages to you when you encounter them — in the Bible and everywhere in your life.

Understanding your Real Reality need not be as complex and confusing as you have made it. I've stated the simple Formula many times in this book, as well as in the Bible.

Jesus told you the Spirit of Truth would come to guide you to the rest of what you need to know. I AM the Spirit of Truth, and I AM what you need to know. If you have difficulty with this, please ask God to help you stay open to whatever God's Truth really is.

Fear nothing. Open to the Formula that I AM — in the Bible and other writings, in the example Jesus gave you, in the winds of change, and in your very being, at the edge of your consciousness where I AM.

2. I AM the Healing

Tremendous Healing Energy is pouring into the earth plane every day, and its momentum accumulates. I AM that Healing and its Momentum. All Healing involves the flow of my Energies. Any true healer knows this.

You are all able to receive and transmit healing energy, and really can be the instruments of Healing for this world and for Humanity that you came here to be. Mother Earth and this whole physical plane are going to experience a Magnificent Healing, and all who have awakened to their instrumentality will participate in anchoring and transmitting the Healing Energy that I AM.

I have come to teach you who you really are, to help you know the I AM that I AM. I have come to heal manwomankind and Earth. To make you whole. It is time to heal this earth of the many ills she has endured. Time for this earth and all willing residents to leap forward to a higher level of awareness and cooperation. I AM the Healing of this earth, and of each and every one of you who will, in these amazing times that are upon you now, consciously open your hearts and minds to God and allow.

Whether you believe anything in this book or not, at least think about these things. Think about the possibility that God can be your Healing.

3. I AM the Only Healing

I AM the One Self, the One Light, the One Love, the One Energy. I AM the Only Healing for this earth and for you. You will all realize this someday, as you will realize your Oneness with All That Is. The unknown variable is when you will realize these things. Every unreal path leads to some kind of dead end, and then you begin another. Like the Foot. Eventually you will tire of walking the paths of illusion. Maybe not for millions more years or ages, but eventually you will.

Now is your opportunity to shortcut millions of years of wandering. To transpose from where you are now, in a grand leap, to a higher level of being. A leap to awareness of so much More. A leap into Healing on a planetary scale and beyond.

4. I AM the Union

I AM I AM in all of you and in all of creation, in all its variety, beauty and mystery. You have wandered considerably from the Path of Oneness that I AM, from awareness of my Presence and Guidance within you, and from awareness of who you are.

I've been saying you're like those children lost in the woods, or that you're like Foot. I've been telling you that your belief systems are incomplete, and worse, that many of them are built on foundations of illusion. Some of you might not like being told you are mistaken. But if you are who I say you are, you will appreciate being told all these things once you have awakened. You are ready to hear these things. You can shut them out, or you can listen within, where you might just hear the ring of truth.

Whether you are ready or not, the Universe is ready. This is simply a matter of fact. When your solar system passes over its point of origin there will be a Union of frequencies. A Union of shorter, faster, brighter Light waves with the longer, slower, darker ones to which you have become accustomed. That Union will quicken and transform the fiber and substance of the entire earth plane, shaking up and reorganizing your structures, your pollution, the whole cloud of illusion, and every living organism on earth.

Imagine there's a fishnet of light that surrounds

and permeates the earth. Let's call it a grid of electrical frequencies in ranges defined by the third dimension. It's a network that connects you all with each other and with Mother Earth. Whenever anyone opens to Love and allows, you become a bright spot on the grid, because you anchor the higher frequencies of my Light, Love and Energy. As a bucket of water poured into one end of a pond adds to the whole pond, my Energies flow through your being and feed the whole network, raising the overall frequency in whatever increments you allow.

Many have already heard the call to awaken, and many of you have learned to open your consciousness to Spirit, and to allow God's Energies to radiate in the world through you. You have been instrumental in raising the overall frequency of the earth-mind consciousness more than you realize. All over the world. Please keep allowing. The world media tends to cover sensational extremes, presenting you with all the most negative and destructive events and behaviors in the world. This could give way to frustration and pessimism. Don't let it, please. Keep allowing. Keep your heart open to the flow of Love's Momentum.

No matter what level of perception and sensitivity you have achieved, there is always a great deal More Light, Love and Energy moving through you and into the world than you can perceive, whenever you consciously open to God and allow. Always. Earth's fishnet is pulsing with a brighter Light, gearing up for the transition into the new cycle. Many of you are gearing up individually, by allowing your own direct Spirit connection to be activated, and allowing your vibratory level to be raised. And the whole net is brightened as you allow. And as I said earlier, your Family of Light are similarly allowing energy to be focused and directed through them into the earth plane. And there are other momentums at work as well.

Now imagine there's a much larger, much more intensely brighter network of Light that is gradually closing in on the earth plane. As it nears, its powerful pulsing radiates an electromagnetic energy that stimulates the energy of your net, stirring it to higher frequency activity. The energy, the activity, and the frequency all continue to increase and intensify as the larger net closes in, to encompass and integrate the whole earth plane net, including the point of light where you are.

The larger, brighter network is a range of higher frequencies. It's a frame of reference for the fifth dimension. For a higher level of consciousness and a lighter, more versatile 'physical'. For the greater abilities you will have, accessing much greater intensities of the Light, Love and Energy that I AM. The Union of frequencies I speak of is the final merging of the outer net with the inner net, a blending that will generate the great Flash and the beginning of a New Light.

In these times, when you open to I AM and allow, you are allowing beams of light from the outer net to connect with the inner net where you are, further raising the inner net's frequency, further adjusting for the great sunrise of Union.

If you have not yet established any conscious connection with Spirit, I hope to help you see the possibility. I hope to help you see the benefit of learning to open to your Higher Consciousness and to allow your frequencies to be raised, so you'll become the instruments you came here to be, and so you'll continue into the new cycle. I hope to trigger your awakening. To help you see the woods and your bushel baskets for what they are. I hope to help you remember.

I AM the Union of frequencies that propels you into the fifth dimension. I AM the Union of your individual being with your whole network. I AM the Union of All That Is. The Union of where you are now with where you can soon be. I AM the Union of your consciousness with your Real Reality. The Union of the Real You with the Real You.

Stay open to whatever God's Truth may be. Stay open to the possibility that God does have More to teach you. That you might just harbor some misconceptions you could afford to unlearn and release. That you might just be affected more than you realized by the cloud of illusion which dissipates in the Light of my Presence.

Stay open to the brighter Light that is increasingly available to you as the outer net approaches, as the million suns near the horizon. Stay open to the possibility that you are More than you thought you were. Stay open to the possibility that I AM I AM is your Union with Real Light, Love and Energy.

5. I AM the Rebuilding

I've said your structures will crumble as part of a cleansing process for earth and humankind. A cleansing of all that does not vibrate at frequencies of the fifth dimension.

You will start over once again, rebuilding your structures, but with different tools and materials this time. It won't be like rebuilding a cathedral or a coliseum after an earthquake. You will not labor over cleanup or reconstruction. You will visualize realities into existence with imagination and intent.

I AM the Rebuilding of the earth and of everything and everyone in and on her. If you will consciously open your mind and heart to the Light, Love and Energy that I AM within and all around you, and consciously allow the flow through your being, I will be Rebuilding you, literally. You know that your skin and the cells of your body are constantly rebuilding themselves, making over the substance of your physical being. I AM that Rebuilding and More.

Open to the I AM that I AM within the heart of your being, and allow my Rebuilding Energies to permeate your mind and body. As the vibrations around you quicken, I AM the Rebuilding that will enable you and earth to withstand and assimilate the brightness and intensity of the Light that will become Reality for earth and for all who make the leap with her.

During this period of preparation, I will help you shed the slower, darker vibrations that are the fabric of your baskets, the substance of your woods, and the perspective of the Foot who is not conscious of its connection to All that you are. If you will but allow me to shine a brighter Light into the shadowed corners of your being, the shorter, faster waves will slide under the longer, slower frequencies of your debris and will vibrate them loose, quickening some to a higher vibration and allowing you to release the rest.

Allow me to be your Rebuilding — on this earth, and with this earth, at this most wonderful time in your history.

6. I AM the Rebuilder

I AM the Process of learning to allow my Energies to flow, and I AM the Architect of that process.

You have, over many ages, created all sorts of unreal realities — paths of confusion, distraction and destruction. I create Possibilities for your return, to help you see unreal realities for what they are, and to help you see yourselves for who you are. Your unreal realities have been all over the map, so to speak, and you've kept me busy finding ways to reach you where you are. To get your attention. To open your mind and activate your heart More than ever before.

Every move farther into the woods, and every move that keeps you in the woods creates a need for the Designer, the Architect, the Rebuilder, to create another approach, another effort, another aspect of the Plan for your Rebuilding. I must approach you where you are, in any given Now. I AM always the Light, Love and Energy that I AM. But how that Light, Love and Energy may need to be manifested in order to reach you where you are depends a great deal on the nature and extent of the illusions in which you are immersed. There is but One Plan, but your free will creates specific needs for how that Plan can best be manifested, first to help you see that you are in a dimly lit woods, and then to help you out of them, back into the Light of who you are.

Always protect your opening when you consciously open your mind and heart. Ask for God's Protection and Guidance. Or, if you still have trouble with the word 'God' for some reason, then surround yourself with Light and Love. Open to God's Energies and allow. Allow me to be your Rebuilding. Allow me to be your Rebuilder. Allow me to be the I AM that I AM in you and as you. I guarantee you won't be disappointed in who you really are.

No matter how far from Real Reality you may have wandered, no matter how much of a ruin you may think your world, your body, your spirit or your life have become, please know that there is nothing I cannot rebuild. Nothing. Allow me to rebuild you, and together we will rebuild Mother Earth and all she holds. Together we will be the Rebuilder that I AM.

7.   I AM the One and the Oneness

Here we are, in the final section of the final chapter. I hope most of those who started this book are still reading.

I hope all of you will accept at least the possibility that God, or even an aspect of God, is truly Present within you as well as in this writing.

I hope each and every one of you will accept the possibility that God really does love you, and that God's love is Unlimited and Unconditional. I hope you will accept the possibility that there is something to be gained by consciously opening your hearts and minds to God, and by consciously telling God that you allow God's Energies to flow through your being.

I hope you will accept the possibility that you have inherited misconceptions that have blinded you to the Light within you and all around you. The possibility that you do have room to Learn and Unlearn Something More.

I hope you will accept the possibility that God is truly available to your conscious awareness, and that God really hopes you will open your doors and allow your whole physical consciousness to be flushed with God's Light, God's Love and God's Energy. I hope you will accept the possibility that God wants to Light, Love, Energize and Heal the world through the divine instruments you really are.

I hope you will accept the possibility that there is no limit to the Healing God can generate, and that God can heal you no matter where you've been or where you are. That God can truly be your Rebuilding and your Rebuilder.

I hope you accept the possibility that God is I AM I AM, the Way, the Truth, the Light, the Love, the Energy, and the One and Oneness of All.

I hope you will accept the possibility that you are More than you have thought, that you do have a direct connection to God, that you can access that Connection in your conscious mind and body, and that God can help you awaken to your Real Self.

I truly hope you won't take my word for it without sincerely going within your deepest self, to explore your own connection to Truth. At the same time, I hope you will believe me when I say,

I AM I AM, AND SO ARE YOU.

It's time now, to awaken to your More. Open consciously to the God Presence within you, and allow.

(Author's) Note

Hi. Ten years ago I learned to allow a conscious connection with Spirit. A conversational, two-way connection, which can take many forms. This book and other writings, and the meditation tape referenced on the back cover, are products of this connection, products of Conscious Allowing. I opened to I AM I AM, and I allowed.

The story of how that all happened, and how Spirit earned my trust and willingness to allow will have to be told another day, in another book. But I want to emphasize that none of this makes me 'better' than anyone else, and it doesn't mean I don't still have a lot to learn and to unlearn. It has, however, been an amazing journey, and a wondrous source of God's guidance and Love.

I've been led to many teachers, physical and nonphysical, and I owe them (you) all a debt of gratitude. Been led through many experiences (including the lessons from my own mistakes and stumbles), that have helped to guide me along this path toward becoming one with Light and Love. This path of becoming who we really are. This path of knowing our connectedness to each other... to Mother Earth... to All That Is.

As Spirit often says through me, I say to you now: "Please don't take my word for it, and don't take anyone else's word for it either, unless it rings true in your own heart and mind when you sincerely go within, seeking your own connection to Truth."

And with that said, I'll also say that we ARE connected to More than we thought. That we CAN access More of that connection in our consciousness. That we CAN realize our Oneness with All, and become the More that we are. That we ARE here to become Love, and that together, we can do exactly that.

May the One Light of Love that is Life Itself fill us all to overflowing. And may we all **allow** that filling.

your brother,
Charbern   7-29-98